LITTLE TALKS
ABOUT
GOD & YOU

V. GILBERT BEERS

ILLUSTRATED BY JAN CIELOHA

HARVEST HOUSE PUBLISHERS
Eugene, Oregon 97402

LITTLE TALKS ABOUT GOD AND YOU

Copyright © 1986 by Harvest House Publishers
Eugene, Oregon 97402

Library of Congress Catalog Card Number 86-080707
ISBN 0-89081-519-4

Printed in the United States of America.

FOR PARENTS AND TEACHERS

When I was a boy on an Illinois farm, there was something special about a summer evening. With dinner and dishwashing done, the entire family went to the front porch and talked the evening away. That was another era. When our children were in the growing-up years, we did not have entire evenings to talk. They were busy in orchestras, little leagues, homework, and a dozen other things. Our evenings were filled with activity too.

The old farmhouse is gone now, and with it has passed a wonderful family experience. We live in another era now, when few people could hope to spend entire evenings talking as a family.

But with our children we have had hundreds of *little* talks, some only five or ten minutes, and some longer. We have talked of many things—of the days when Indians lived in our backyard, of hurts and problems which our children brought home from school, and of all the little things they encountered on their pilgrimage through life. The most special times have been our little talks about God, and where He fits into their lives and ours.

Consistently through the years, my wife, Arlie, brought out the storybooks before bedtime and read with drama and flourish to our wide-eyed children. It was an everyday sight to see her sitting there with children wrapped around her as she and they literally wore the covers off favorite books. Of course, this reading always prompted little talks, too.

Arlie and I have deliberately looked for every excuse we could find to stop and have a little talk with our children. One-on-one times were the best, because then we could really get into the child's head and heart. We've had little talks sprawled on the floor, or draped over a sofa, or sitting on a log in the woods, or hiking a trail, or in a canoe, or at a dozen or two other favorite haunts.

Little talks were almost never planned—they just happened. Yet in these wonderful brief encounters we cultivated lasting friendships with our children. Now they are grown, and they are truly our best friends. And often they are our most honest counselors.

Frequently parents or teachers think a good talk must be a long talk. More often the opposite is true—five-minute talks can bear wonderful fruit. The prerequisite is that during those five minutes you must truly be with your child, and not let your heart or mind be elsewhere. If you talk grudgingly, you will not talk productively.

In this book you will find little talks which will take from five minutes to as long as you want to talk. If you read one each day with your child, and talk about it, you will see wonderful things begin to happen in your relationship. It's a five-minute lifebuilding exercise, and it will be pure fun, too.

These are little talks about great truths, but great truths made simple. In a very real sense they involve you in a special time with you, your child, and God. Your child learns that these times for little talks are times of delight when he or she will get to know you and God a little better each day.

Younger children will also enjoy reading this book, for it is written in a simple style designed to make reading easy. When they do, these everyday situations will encourage them to have little talks with God or you.

Be sure to get acquainted with the Topical Guide and Biblical Guide in the back of this book. They will help you find the little talk that you need in order to answer that special urgent question.

Invest five minutes or more with your child each day. There is no more rewarding investment to be made. The dividends are wonderful, and they are eternal.

—V. Gilbert Beers

LITTLE TALKS
ABOUT
GOD & YOU

The Balloon Man

One day the balloon man walked into the park with a hundred balloons. "Come and get your free balloon!" he said to the children there. But only two boys and two girls came to get a free balloon. The others thought something was wrong, so they would not do it. Soon the balloon man walked sadly from the park with 96 balloons.

A Little Talk about Something Free

1. How did the man feel when he walked away with all those balloons? Who did he want to give them to?
2. How would you feel if you had a special gift for someone but that person would not take it?

Jesus is like the balloon man. He came to give each of us a life that goes on forever. He offers each of us a room in His beautiful home in heaven. But only a few people accept His wonderful offer. How do you think Jesus feels about that?

A Little Talk about Jesus and You

1. What special gift does Jesus want to give you? He wants you to live with Him forever, doesn't He?
2. How do you think Jesus feels when someone will not take His free gift? Have you accepted His free gift? If you haven't, would you like to do that now?

BIBLE READING: John 10:27-29.
BIBLE TRUTH: Jesus gives us a life that never ends. John 10:28.
PRAYER: Dear Jesus, thank You for Your wonderful gift of a life that never ends. Thank You for giving me a room in Your wonderful home in heaven. I want to live with You there forever. Amen.

The Face in the Pond

When Laura smiled at the face in the pond, the face smiled back at her. When she frowned, the face in the pond frowned back at her.

"That face in the pond does what I do," said Laura.

"That's because it is a reflection," said Father. "It's like what you see in a mirror. You see yourself bounced back at you."

"The pond and the mirror can only bounce back the way I look," said Laura. "It can't bounce back the way I really am."

"That's true," said Father, "but the Bible tells us about another kind of mirror that can bounce back the way you really are."

A Little Talk about Reflections

1. What was Laura seeing in the pond? Would she see the same thing in a mirror?
2. Father said that something else would show her how she really is inside. Do you know what it is?

"There's a verse in the Bible that tells us about another mirror," said Father. "It tells us that water reflects a face, but it's your heart that reflects the way you really are."

"Yesterday my heart was sad," said Laura.

"Was it telling me something?"

"Yes, it was telling you that you may have done something wrong," said Father, "or that someone hurt you."

"I said something mean to my best friend at school," said Laura.

"Then your heart was like that face in the pond," said Father. "Your heart frowned at you because you did something you should not have done."

"I guess I should watch my heart like I watch my face in the pond," said Laura.

A Little Talk about Jesus and You

1. What does your heart tell you when you do something wrong? What does it tell you when you do something good?
2. If your heart is sad, ask why. Ask Jesus to help you do something good about it.

BIBLE READING: Proverbs 27:19.
BIBLE TRUTH: Your heart reflects the real you in the same way a pond reflects your face. From Proverbs 27:19.
PRAYER: Dear Jesus, help me know when I do something wrong so I can change it. And help me smile inside when I please You. Amen.

Where Did Puppy Come From?

Fluffy barked three happy little barks before she caught the ball. "Good Fluffy!" said Mark. "You are such a smart little dog!"

Mark let Fluffy keep the ball this time. Mother had brought lemonade to the back-yard, where he and Fluffy were playing.

"Where did we get Fluffy?" Mark asked Mother between sips of lemonade.

"From the Millers," said Mother. "They had Fluffy's mother. Before that they even had Fluffy's grandmother."

"Did Fluffy's grandmother have a grand-mother?" asked Mark. "And did that grandmother have a grandmother?"

"I suppose so," said Mother. "There must be grandmothers and grandfathers back to the time of the first Fluffy."

"But where did the first Fluffy come from?" asked Mark.

A Little Talk about Creation

1. Do you know where the first Fluffy came from? What should Mother say to Mark?
2. How do we know who made the first Fluffy? Where can we find the answer?

"God made the first Fluffy," said Mother. "There is no animal on earth without grandmothers and grandfathers, and great-great-great grandmothers and grandfathers. But God made the first animal of every kind."

Mark sipped his lemonade. "That's what my Sunday school teacher said last Sunday," said Mark. "We had a lesson about God making all the animals. I'm glad God made Fluffy's first great-great-great-grandmother. That makes Fluffy more special than ever."

"And that makes you special too," said Mother. "God created your great-great-great-grandmother too."

A Little Talk about God and You

1. Do you have a pet dog or cat? Have you ever wondered about its great-great-great-grandmother or grandfather?
2. How do we know that God made the first dogs and cats? Have you ever thanked Him for making your pet?

BIBLE READING: Genesis 1:20-25.
BIBLE TRUTH: God created every living animal. From Genesis 1:21,25.
PRAYER: Dear God, thank You for making puppies and kitties. They are special, and so are You for doing this. Amen.

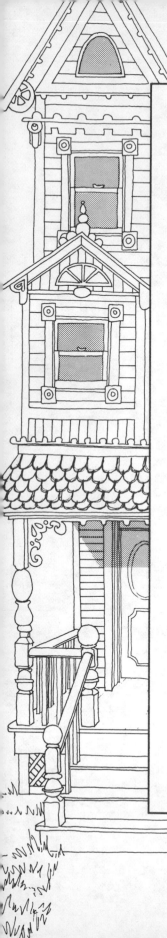
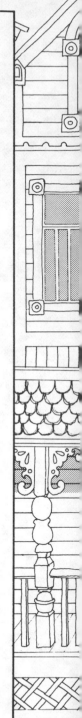

My House

Jennifer was ashamed of her house. There was nothing wrong with it, but it was an old house. It looked like something from a storybook that Grandma had when she was a little girl.

That's why she began to make excuses when Amy came in for a drink of water. Amy looked here and she looked there. But she didn't say anything for a while.

"My house is probably not a nice new house like yours," said Jennifer.

Jennifer's mother heard what she said.

A Little Talk about Your House and Mine

1. What do you think Amy should say? What do you think Mother will say? What would you say?
2. Are you ever ashamed to have a friend into your house? Let's see what happened to Jennifer.

Amy looked here and there in Jennifer's house. "Wow!" she said at last. "Would I love to live here!"

"You . . . you would?" Jennifer asked.

"Your house is like something in my wonderful old storybooks," said Amy. "I could pretend that I was living with my favorite characters."

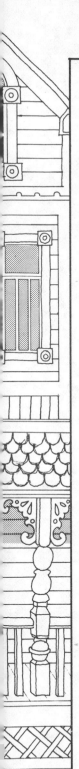

Jennifer's mother smiled, but said nothing.

"And your house is so clean and neat," said Amy. "Our house is new, but it's not as clean and neat as yours. I . . . I guess I would be ashamed to take you into my house after seeing yours."

Jennifer stayed behind in the house when Amy went out to play. "Thank you for such a wonderful house," Jennifer said to Mother. "I guess I never thought about how hard you work to keep it clean and neat."

Mother gave Jennifer a big hug. Then Jennifer ran out to play. From now on she would be glad to bring her friends into her wonderful old storybook house.

A Little Talk about Jesus and You

1. If you are ever ashamed of your house, ask why. Then ask what you can do.
2. Think of some good things about your house. Have you ever thanked Mother and Father for giving you a good house? Have you ever thanked Jesus?

BIBLE READING: Hebrews 3:2-4.
BIBLE TRUTH: The builder is greater than the house. The parents and children are more important than the house itself. From Hebrews 3:3.
PRAYER: Dear Jesus, I love my parents more than my house. But I thank You for each. Help me take care of my house and be grateful for it. Amen.

A Smiling Face

Carol looked at the envelope that Mother had received in the mail. On the back was a big yellow dot with a smiling face on it.

"Why do people put smiling faces on envelopes?" Carol asked Mother.

A Little Talk about Cheerfulness

1. Have you seen these little yellow smiling faces? Why do you think someone puts one on an envelope?
2. Would you rather see a sad face or a smiling face? Why?
3. What do you think Mother will tell Carol?

"Perhaps a yellow smiling face like this is another way of sending a smile through the mail," said Mother. "Does it make you want to smile too?"

Carol looked at the smiling face again. Then she began to smile. "It does," she said.

"When you smile, it makes a friend want to smile too," said Mother. "But when you frown, it can make your friends sad too. Jesus wants His friends to be cheerful, don't you think?"

A Little Talk about Jesus and You

1. Why should Christians have smiling faces? Why are we so happy?
2. Have you smiled for Jesus today? Do you look happy and smile because you love Him?

BIBLE READING: Proverbs 15:13,15,30.
BIBLE TRUTH: A cheerful look brings joy to those who see you. From Proverbs 15:30.
PRAYER: Dear Jesus, as I look at this little yellow smiling face, help me remember to show others how cheerful I am. When someone wants to know why, help me to tell them about You. Amen.

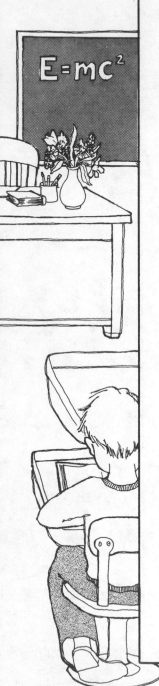

Sharing Is Fun

Two boys went to school one day. One forgot his lunch, so he had nothing to eat. The other boy brought his lunch. He had two sandwiches, an apple, a pear, and four cookies.

At lunchtime the first boy stayed behind in the classroom to read a book. The second boy went down to the lunchroom to eat his two sandwiches, an apple, a pear, and four cookies.

A Little Talk about Sharing

1. What did the first boy have to eat for lunch? What did the second boy have to eat for lunch?
2. If you were the first boy with the lunch, what would you do about the second boy without a lunch?

$E = mc^2$

Lunchroom

When the boy with the lunch saw his friend stay in the classroom, he came back to talk with him. Then he learned that his friend had forgotten his lunch.

So the boy who had his lunch had a pear, one sandwich, and two cookies. The boy who forgot his lunch had an apple, one sandwich, and two cookies. And both boys had a happy time eating together.

A Little Talk about Jesus and You

1. Why do you think the boy who forgot his lunch was happy as he ate? Why do you think the boy who remembered his lunch was happy while he ate?
2. Why do you think Jesus was happy to watch the two boys eat their lunch?

BIBLE READING: Matthew 6:2-4.
BIBLE TRUTH: Share with God's people who have need. From Romans 12:13.
PRAYER: You have shared so much with me, dear Jesus. Help me to share happily with others so that I may please You and be like You. Amen.

Good Fruit

"What a beautiful apple tree!" said Chris. "It has so many bright red apples on it!"

Father smiled. "Good apples come from good apple trees," he said. "But look at that other apple tree."

Chris looked at the tree. It was not a good tree. Its branches were cracked. Some were hanging down, and their leaves were withered.

"What kind of apples do you see on this tree?" Father asked Chris.

A Little Talk about Good Fruit

1. What kind of apples were on the good tree? What kind of apples do you think Chris saw on the bad tree?
2. Why doesn't a bad tree give good fruit? Do you expect good things to come from a bad person? Why not?

"Good trees usually give good fruit," Father told Chris. "And bad trees usually give bad fruit. Bad trees seldom give good fruit."

"Is that like people?" Chris asked.

"That's what Jesus said," Father told Chris. "When you accept Jesus as your Savior, your life is like a good tree, a Jesus tree. If your life is a Jesus tree, it will grow Jesus fruit."

"I want my life to be a Jesus tree," said Chris.

A Little Talk about Jesus and You

1. Have you asked Jesus to come into your life? If you have, you can let your life be like a beautiful tree for Him. If you haven't, would you like to do that now?
2. What kind of fruit can you give for Jesus?

BIBLE READING: Matthew 7:16-20.
BIBLE TRUTH: A good tree bears good fruit and a bad tree bears bad fruit. From Matthew 7:17.
PRAYER: Lord, make my life like a good fruit tree so that I may give Your good fruit to other people. Amen.

Nobody Loves Me

Mother knew that Jan had not had a good day at school. Mothers have a way of knowing those things. Perhaps it was the way Jan closed the door when she came home from school. Or it may have been the way Jan pouted.

Whatever it was, Mother knew this had been a bad day at school. "Want to tell me about it?" Mother asked.

"Nobody loves me," said Jan.

"Nobody?" Mother asked.

A Little Talk about Love

1. Have you ever said that nobody loved you? Did you find out that somebody loved you after all?
2. What would you say to Jan if you were Mother? Can you think of someone who loves her?

"Let's look at something together," said Mother.

Mother poured a glass of milk for Jan and one for herself. Then she put a little plate of cookies on the table in the kitchen.

Jan almost smiled when Mother sat down with her and began to munch a cookie. Jan did smile when Mother opened the family photo album.

"Here we are at our last picnic," said Mother. "I think you had fun there, didn't you?"

"That was so much fun!" said Jan. "I just love our family picnics."

"Well, now, here is a picture of Father carrying you around the table," said Mother. "Do you think Father loves you?"

Jan smiled. "Yes, I know he does," she said.

"And here I am, giving you a sandwich," said Mother. "Do you think I love you?"

Jan nodded her head "Yes." Then Mother pointed to Jan's big brother. Jan knew that he loved her too. Before long Jan had seen pictures of two cousins, a favorite aunt and uncle, Grandpa and Grandma, and her Sunday school teacher. And everyone loved her! Jan said so.

"I. . .I guess I was wrong," said Jan. "Lots of people love me."

"Including Jesus!" said Mother.

A Little Talk about Jesus and You

1. Jan learned that many people loved her. Make a list of people who love you.
2. Does your list include Jesus? How do you know that Jesus loves you?

BIBLE READING: 1 John 4:19-21.
BIBLE TRUTH: We love other people because Jesus loved us first. From 1 John 4:19.
PRAYER: Dear Jesus, thank You for loving me. Help me to love others too. Amen.

What Do the Stars Say?

"There must be a million stars tonight," Todd said to Mother and Father.

Todd tried to count them, but when he got to a hundred, he could not tell where he was.

"Have you heard them?" Father asked.

Todd looked surprised. "Stars don't talk," he said.

"The Bible says they do," said Father.

A Little Talk about the Stars

1. Have you ever been camping in a wonderful place like this? Have you seen the Milky Way? Have you seen a night sky filled with stars?
2. What do you think Father means when he says the stars talk?

"Let me read something from the Bible," said Father. So he read Psalm 19:1-4. This is what it says:

The heavens declare the glory of God;
the skies proclaim the work of his hands.
Day after day they pour forth speech;
night after night they display knowledge.
There is no speech or language
where their voice is not heard.
Their voice goes out into all the earth,

their words to the ends of the world.

"The stars do not speak English or French or Spanish or German," said Father. "But the sky full of stars, the sun, the moon, the clouds, and the colors of the sunset say something wonderful to us."

"What do they say?" asked Todd.

"Praise the Lord!" said Father. "All that He has made says 'Praise the Lord!' "

A Little Talk about God and You

1. Why should we praise God? Should we praise Him for the stars? Should we praise Him for the clouds? For the rainbow? For the sunset? For the sun and moon?
2. The wonderful sky and all that is in it seems to say "Praise the Lord!" Remember this the next time you look at the clouds or the stars.

BIBLE READING: Psalm 19:1-4.
BIBLE TRUTH: From the sunrise to the sunset, let the name of the Lord be praised. From Psalm 113:3.
PRAYER: Let me praise You, Lord, for everything I see in the sky. And let me give praise for You, because You made everything there. Amen.

Does God Know What We are Thinking?

"This is an exciting book!" said Keith. "It's about a man who knows what other people are thinking. Can you do that? Do you know what I am thinking?" Keith asked his mother.

Mother smiled. "How could I know that?" she asked. "Only God knows that."

Keith was quiet for a moment. "Does God really know what I am thinking?" he asked. "Does He know each thought that I have?"

A Little Talk about What God Knows

1. Do you know what your friends are thinking before they say it? Of course not. Not one friend or family member knows that.
2. But did you know that God knows every thought you think? The Bible tells us that.

Mother opened her Bible to Psalm 139 and read the first four verses. "Before a word is on my tongue, you know it completely, O Lord," she read.

"I think I'll be a little more careful about what I think," said Keith.

Mother smiled. "Our minds are like TV screens that God can watch," she said. "So we should be more careful what we put on the screen."

That's a good idea, isn't it?

A Little Talk about God and You

1. God knows what you say or pray before you open your mouth. That's how much He cares for you.
2. Have you ever prayed silently, without opening your mouth? God still hears you! Do you pray aloud sometimes, talking to Him? He likes that too.

BIBLE READING: Psalm 139:1-4.
BIBLE TRUTH: Before I say a word, the Lord knows what I am thinking. From Psalm 139:4.
PRAYER: Dear Lord, help me to think thoughts that please You. Thank you for making so many beautiful things for me to think about. Amen.

Don't Walk, the Light is Red!

"Stop, Denny, the light is red!" Katie shouted. Denny had not even bothered to look at the light. Katie screamed as a car slammed on its brakes. The driver opened his window and shouted at Denny.

"Didn't you see the red light?" asked Katie.

"I didn't even see the light," said Denny. "I was thinking about the TV program I saw last night."

Katie shook her finger at Denny. "You've got to be responsible for yourself!" she shouted. Do you think Katie is right?

A Little Talk about Being Responsible

1. What does being responsible mean?
2. Why must each of us be responsible for ourselves? Is someone going to keep you from doing every foolish thing you want to do? Can you ask God to keep you from doing foolish things like walking when the light is red?

Denny smiled at Katie. "I should be angry at you for shouting at me," he said. "But I'm not. You're right. I was careless. I could have been hurt or even killed."

Denny and Katie talked about other ways that boys and girls should be responsible. Before long they were safely home. But they had a long list. Each of them planned to hang it in their rooms.

A Little Talk About God and You

1. Do you think that God wants to protect you from harm?
2. Do you think He wants to protect you when you do something foolish that could hurt you? How can you do your part to help God take care of you?

BIBLE READING: Romans 14:12.
BIBLE TRUTH: Each of us will have to explain to God what we have done. From Romans 14:12.
PRAYER: Dear Lord, You have told me to be careful of the things I do, because I will have to explain why I did some of them. Help me to do what You want me to do. Then when I explain what I have done, it will make sense. Amen.

Who Did It?

"I think Bert broke that window," said Kelly. "He is just the type who would do that."

"Did you see him do it?" asked Mother.

"No," said Kelly, "but he could have done it."

"Did someone else see him do it?" asked Father.

"No," said Kelly, "but who else would do it?"

"Were his footprints out there, or did he leave something behind at the window?" asked Mother.

"No," said Kelly, "but I think he did it."

"What would you think if Bert said all of these things about you?" asked Father.

A Little Talk about Judging Others

1. Why does Kelly think Bert broke the window? What's wrong with that?
2. Is Kelly judging Bert without a good reason?

"Jesus said you should not say those things about Bert," said Mother.

Kelly looked surprised. "I don't remember Jesus talking about me in the Bible," she said.

"He didn't say your name," said Mother, "but you can put it in the right place."

Mother read this from her Bible: "Do not judge, or you too will be judged. For in the same way you judge others, you will be judged."

"That's from Matthew 7:1,2," said Mother. "Now let's put your name in."

Then Mother read the verses again. "Kelly should not judge, or Kelly will be judged. For in the same way Kelly judges others, Kelly will be judged."

"Wow, do you think Jesus really meant for my name to be in there?" asked Kelly.

"I think He meant for each of us to put our names in there," said Mother.

"I'm sorry I said those things about Bert," said Kelly. "I know now that Jesus does not want me to do that."

A Little Talk about Jesus and You

1. What did Jesus say about judging? What will happen if we judge someone else the wrong way?
2. Have you ever put your name in a Bible verse like this? Try it on some of your favorite Bible verses. It shows how the Bible is especially for you.

BIBLE READING: Matthew 7:1-5.
BIBLE TRUTH: Don't judge others, or you will be judged the same way. From Matthew 7:1,2.
PRAYER: Forgive me, dear Jesus, if I have thought wrong thoughts about others. Amen.

Can You Say You Are Sorry?

It should have been a happy day at the zoo. But things sometimes go wrong. Then what do you do?

Father and Mother had just bought two beautiful balloons for Carla and her bigger brother Gary. There was one balloon for each. But Gary wanted to hold both balloons "just for a minute."

Of course Carla did not want to give up her balloon, even for a minute. But Gary argued and made such a fuss that Carla let him have it.

Mistakes do happen. This was a mistake, for both balloons slipped from Gary's hand. Before he knew what had happened, the balloons were high in the air.

Carla began to cry. Gary stood there so surprised that he said nothing.

Father and Mother were not happy about Gary's foolish mistake. Gary could see that.

"Well, do you want to say something to Carla?" Father asked Gary.

A Little Talk about Saying You Are Sorry

1. Why was this a foolish mistake? What would you say if you were Carla? What should Gary say to Carla?

2. Are you sorry for something you have done this week? Have you said you are sorry? If not, why not now?

"But what should I say?" Gary asked. "I don't have any money to buy her a new balloon."

"Isn't there something else you would like to say?" Father asked.

"I. . .I'm sorry," Gary said to Carla.

Carla smiled. You do think she forgave Gary, don't you?

A Little Talk about Jesus and You

1. When we do something wrong, what should we say to the person we have hurt? Why?
2. When someone tells us he is sorry, what should we do? Why? What would we want Jesus to do if we told Him we are sorry for something?

BIBLE READING: Luke 17:3,4.
BIBLE TRUTH: If your brother does something wrong, tell him about it. If he says he is sorry, forgive him. From Luke 17:3.
PRAYER: Dear Jesus, I want to forgive other people as You have forgiven me. And I want You to forgive me as I forgive others. Amen.

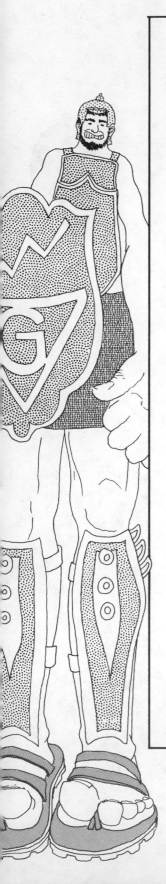

Do You Need a Shield?

When David went to fight Goliath, he met a very big man. Goliath carried a large shield. Whenever someone shot an arrow, Goliath put the shield in front of him and the arrow bounced off it. If someone tried to hit Goliath, he put his shield in front of him and did not get hit.

Shields kept Bible-time soldiers from getting hurt. They protected people from arrows and clubs and spears.

Did you know that God is our shield?

A Little Talk about God's Protection

1. How do you think God is like a shield? What does He protect us from?

2. Can you think of some times you wanted God's protection? Did you ask Him?

God told Abraham, "I am your shield" (Genesis 15:1). Many years later the writer of Psalms said, "The Lord God is a sun and shield" (Psalm 84:11). In other places in the Bible God explains that His truth protects us from Satan's evil arrows and clubs. Psalm 91:4 and Ephesians 6:14 tell us that. Would you like to read them?

A Little Talk about God and You

1. Were you tempted to do something wrong this week? Satan tempts us, doesn't he? Did you ask God to help you?
2. The next time you are tempted to do something wrong, ask God to be your shield against Satan.

BIBLE READING: Ephesians 6:10-18.
BIBLE TRUTH: The Lord will cover you and protect you. His truth will be your shield. From Psalm 91:4.
PRAYER: Dear God, so often I am tempted to do something I should not do. Thank you for protecting me from Satan's arrows of temptation. I'm so glad I can stay close to You, so that You can keep me safe. Amen.

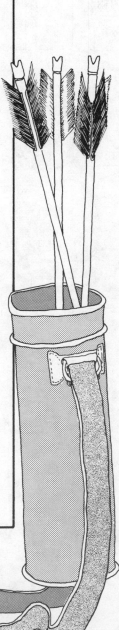

Can You Love a Person Like This?

"Look!" said Father. "The police caught the man who killed that little girl. She was your age, Sarah."

Sarah looked at the man's picture in Father's newspaper. "I hate him! I hate him! I hate him!" she shouted.

Father put his paper down and took Sarah on his lap. "That's what I thought too," he said. "But now I think we should love him. Would you like to talk about it?"

A Little Talk about Love

1. Why does Sarah hate this man? Would you feel the same way? Why?
2. What do you think Father will say to Sarah?

"This man did something terrible," Father said. "Do you think God hates what he did?"

"Yes," Sarah answered. "I know He does."

"God hates what the man did, but does He hate the man?" Father asked. "Would He like to see this man in hell?"

Sarah thought about this. Suddenly she felt sorry for this bad man. "I wouldn't like that," she said. "I wish that man would believe in

Jesus. Then he would not want to hurt people."

Father smiled. "I'm glad you said that," he told Sarah. "God loves this man too. He would like to see this man believe in Jesus. Then the man would be sorry for the bad things that he has done. He would do good things for Jesus."

"Why don't we pray for that man right now?" Sarah asked. "Let's ask God to send someone to tell him about Jesus."

Sarah and Father prayed. They asked that someone would tell this man about Jesus.

A Little Talk about Jesus and You

1. Is it all right to hate something bad that a person has done? Is it all right to hate that person? Why not?
2. Why did Sarah feel sorry for this man? What did Sarah ask Jesus to do? Why?
3. Are you angry at someone? Have you wanted to see that person hurt in some way? What would Jesus want? What should you ask Jesus to do?

BIBLE READING: Colossians 3:12-14.
BIBLE TRUTH: Get rid of things like anger and hatred. From Colossians 3:8.
PRAYER: Dear Jesus, I'm glad that You forgive bad people when they ask You. I'm sorry when I want to see someone hurt. Please forgive me, and forgive that person for what he has done. Amen.

God's TV Cameras

Anne was quiet as she watched the news on TV. "They must have a good camera," Anne said at last.

"Why do you say that?" Father asked.

"Because they just took pictures in England, then down south, then out west, then in our city," said Anne. "That's a good camera that can be everywhere at once."

"They have more than one camera," said Father. "There's one in each place. But there is one TV camera that can take pictures everywhere at once."

A Little Talk about Being Everywhere at Once

1. Have you ever wondered how the TV camera can be in so many places in such a short time?
2. What TV camera is Father talking about? What do you think Father will say to Anne about this?

"God can see everywhere at once," said Father. "If you are doing something good at school, He sees that too."

"What if I don't want God to see what I'm doing?" said Anne.

"He still sees it," said Father. "Whenever you think about doing something bad, remember that God is watching you."

A Little Talk about God and You

1. Are you glad God can see all the good things you do? Are you sad when He sees you do something wrong?
2. Why not ask God to help you do more things that please Him? Then help God to help you!

BIBLE READING: Proverbs 15:3.
BIBLE TRUTH: The Lord sees everywhere, watching good people and bad. From Proverbs 15:3.
PRAYER: Dear Lord, I know that You see everything I do. So remind me to do what You want. Amen.

How Far?

Two boys looked at the stars one night.

"God seems a million miles away," said one boy.

"No," said the other. "I think He seems close enough to touch."

Which boy is right?

A Little Talk about How Far

1. How far is the farthest star? God is there, isn't He? He made each star, no matter how far away.
2. How near is God when He touches you and listens to your prayers? He made you and will stay with you.

God is as far as the farthest star and also as near as your heartbeat. So He can touch the farthest star while He touches you. He can listen to the prayers of someone in Africa or Korea or Guatemala while you pray to Him wherever you are.

A Little Talk about God and You

1. God is everywhere at the same time. Is He with you while He is with a missionary in Japan?
2. How far away is God? Can He touch you and hear you? Can He touch the the farthest star at the same time?

BIBLE READING: Jeremiah 23:23,24.
BIBLE TRUTH: God is everywhere, so He can see anything, even you, all the time. From Jeremiah 23:24.
PRAYER: Thank You, God, for being with me all the time. While You keep the stars in place, You stay by my side. Amen.

GOD
one million
miles away

Keeping Promises

"I'll come over to your house after school tomorrow. That's a promise," Marie told her friend Debra. "I'll be there no matter what happens."

"What if it's raining hard?" Mother asked Marie later. "Or what if you get sick?"

"Well, then I won't go," said Marie.

"But you promised that you would go," said Mother. "Do you know what a promise is?"

A Little Talk about Promises

1. What do you think a promise is? Should you make a promise and then break it? Why not?
2. If you were Mother, what would you have said to Debra?

"A promise is something very special," said Mother. "It says a person can trust you. Many people in the Bible made special promises to God, and then broke them. God said it is better not to make promises than to break them."

"Does God always keep His promises?" asked Marie.

"Yes, the Bible tells us that He does," said Mother. "That means you can trust Him. If He ever broke a promise, you would not be sure. But He has never broken even one promise."

"Then I should be more careful about making promises," said Marie. "And I should be careful not to break promises too."

A Little Talk about God and You

1. Would you trust God if He broke His promises? Why not?
2. Will other people trust you if you break your promises? Why not?
3. Why should we be careful about the promises we make?

BIBLE READING: Joshua 23:14.
BIBLE TRUTH: God keeps every promise. He never breaks even one of them. From Joshua 23:14.
PRAYER: Help me keep my promises, dear God, so I will be like You. Then other people will trust me, as they trust You. Amen.

Whose Footprints Should We Follow?

"Look at the footprints I'm leaving in the snow!" said Grace.

"Bruno sees them," said Father. "And he smells them too. Look at him follow you."

The big German shepherd sniffed at each of Grace's footprints. Then he went on to the next.

"Looks like he's going to follow you wherever you go," said Father.

Grace laughed. "Suppose I walk up a tree," she said. "Would Bruno follow me there?"

A Little Talk about Following

1. Do you think Bruno would walk up a tree after Grace? Why not?
2. What kind of people do you want to follow? Why? What kind of people do you not want to follow? Why not?

"Bruno is too smart for that," said Father. "But often we are not as smart as Bruno. We follow other people into places where we shouldn't go, just because someone else went there first."

"We talked about that at Sunday school last Sunday," said Grace. "The teacher said that we who are Christians should set a good example for the other kids. Maybe some will follow us instead of the kids who are doing wrong things."

"That's a good reason to leave the right kind of footprints by the way you live," said Father.

A Little Talk about Jesus and You

1. Did Jesus set a good example for us? Did He ever do anything wrong?
2. Why does Jesus want us to set a good example for others? How can we do that? What kinds of things should Christians do? What should we not do?

BIBLE READING: Matthew 5:14-16.
BIBLE TRUTH: Be a good example in what you say, think, and do. From 1 Timothy 4:12.
PRAYER: Dear Jesus, You have left good footprints for me to follow. Teach me to leave good footprints for others to follow too. Amen.

Would Jesus Spank Me?

Charles knew it was wrong to tease his little sister, but he did it anyway. Mother had told him many times not to do it.

"If you do that again, I will spank you," Mother told Charles.

Charles thought for a minute. "Jesus wouldn't spank me, would He?" he asked.

A Little Talk about Discipline

1. Would you like to help Mother know what to say? Would Jesus spank us?
2. Think of some kinds of discipline other than spanking. Would Jesus do any of those?

"I can't think of a Bible verse about Jesus spanking someone," said Mother, "but there are verses about Jesus trying to discipline someone."

"What does that mean?" asked Charles.

"Discipline is helping someone stop doing wrong things and start doing right things," said Mother. "Spanking is punishing someone for wrong things. Jesus took a whip and made people stop selling things in God's house. That was discipline. But He didn't really spank them."

"I think Jesus wants to keep us from doing wrong," said Charles. "So that's why He wants mothers and fathers to help Him."

A Little Talk about Jesus and You

1. Would you like Jesus to keep you from doing wrong things? He will help you. Will you ask Him to help?
2. Would you like Jesus to help you do right things? Will you ask Him to do that?

BIBLE READING: John 2:13-16.
BIBLE TRUTH: Jesus is able to keep you from doing what you should not do. From Jude 24.
PRAYER: Dear Jesus, keep me from doing what I should not do. And teach me to do what I should do. And thank You for Mother and Father, who help You take care of me. Amen.

Does an Angel Watch over You?

What would you think if you saw an angel? Would you be afraid? One day an angel came to see Mary. "Greetings!" the angel said to Mary. Mary was really afraid, because this was the first time she had seen an angel. But it wasn't the first time an angel had ever talked to someone. Abraham saw an angel. So did Jacob. He saw a great stairway to heaven filled with angels. Even Balaam saw an angel. You and I may never see one on earth, but there may be one near you right now. Would you like to talk about this?

A Little Talk about Angels

1. Have you ever heard of guardian angels? This means angels who guard you, or watch over you. God sends angels to do this. Read Psalm 91:11.

2. Angels guard people who love Jesus. But they do not keep all bad things from happening to us. They would probably not keep you from getting spanked or getting a thorn in your finger. Sometimes they do not keep us from getting hurt. What do they keep from happening? We do not know exactly. That's a secret between them and God.

from the desk of :
.......God......

Angels are God's special messengers. They run special errands for Him. In Bible times they brought a message that God wanted someone to have. They protected some people and kept them from getting hurt. At certain times they did God's work for Him. They still do.

So don't be afraid of angels. They are God's friends and our friends. Let's thank God for sending them to help us even though we can't see them.

A Little Talk about God and You

1. Does God want to help you? Does He want His angels to help you?
2. What may angels do for you? Would you like to thank God for sending angels to help you?

BIBLE READING: Hebrews 13:1-3.
BIBLE TRUTH: God will send His angels to guard you in all your ways. From Psalm 91:11.
PRAYER: Thank You, dear God, for sending angels to take care of me. Teach me to be careful so they will not need to protect me from foolish things. Amen.

Listen!

Grandpa was reading his newspaper, as grandpas often do. But Fred wanted to ask some questions, as boys often do when grandpas are reading their newspapers.

When Fred asked his first question, Grandpa mumbled something that sounded like "ummph." When Fred asked his second question, Grandpa grunted a little. It sounded a little like "unh hunh." And when Fred asked his third question, Grandpa was so interested in his reading that he didn't even answer.

"Are you listening?" Fred asked Grandpa.

A Little Talk about Listening

1. Do you think Grandpa was listening? Why not?
2. What do you think Fred would like Grandpa to do? What would you do if you were Grandpa?

Grandpa put down his newspaper. "What did you say?" he asked Fred.

"I asked if you were listening," Fred replied.

"I'm sorry," said Grandpa. "I was not listening. I let the newspaper talk louder than you. Please ask your questions again and this time I will listen carefully."

A Little Talk about God and You

1. How often does God listen when you talk to Him? How often would you like Him to listen? Why?
2. Why do you think listening pleases God? How does listening help other people to know what God is like? Can we tell others that God listens if we who are His friends do not listen?

BIBLE READING: Psalm 34:4-6.
BIBLE TRUTH: I will listen while My people are talking. From Isaiah 65:24.
PRAYER: Thank You, Lord, for listening at all times. Thank You for never going to sleep or doing something else while I talk with You. Amen.

Obeying the Right Voice

Allen could not understand how he got lost in the big store. One minute he was with Mother, and the next minute he wasn't. He was sure Mother was somewhere nearby. But where?

Then Allen heard a voice calling. "Allen!" it said. It sounded something like Mother's voice. Allen wasn't sure it was her. Should he answer?

A Little Talk about Obeying the Right Voice

1. What would you do if you were Allen?
2. Are you glad to hear the voice of a family member or a friend in a strange place? Why? Why is that much better than the voice of a stranger?

"Mother, is that you?" Allen answered. "Where are you?"

"Here!" Mother called.

Mother and Allen kept calling to each other until they were together again. "I was glad to hear your voice," said Allen. "But I wasn't sure if I should obey, because it didn't sound like you."

"That's because you don't hear me often in a crowded department store," said Mother.

"But I'm glad you did obey and answer. I might not have found you if you hadn't."

A Little Talk about God and You

1. Would you obey the voice of a stranger? Why not?
2. Are you glad Allen obeyed his mother's voice? Are you glad when you can obey your mother's or father's voice?
3. God speaks to us through the Bible. Do you like to obey His voice?

BIBLE READING: Psalm 29:3-9.
BIBLE TRUTH: Jesus' followers listen to Him because they know His voice. From John 10:4.
PRAYER: Dear Jesus, I want to listen to You speak through Your Word. And I want to do what You tell me. Amen.

Thanking God

"I earned the money for this food," a man said. "Why should I thank God for it?"

"I bought this food at the grocery store," a woman said. "Why should I thank God for it?"

"I worked hard to plant my garden and gather the things that grew there," said another man. "Why should I thank God for them?"

"Mother made dinner for me tonight," a boy said. "Why should I thank God for it?"

A Little Talk about Being Thankful

1. What should you say to each of these people? Why should they thank God for their food?
2. Who earned the money for your food? Have you thanked Mother or Father for that? Who cooks your food for you? Have you thanked Mother or Father for that? Who shopped at the grocery store for your food? Have you thanked Mother or Father for that?
3. Why should you thank God for your food?

Look through your pantry or cabinet where you store your food. Ask Mother to do this with you. Try to find a food that God did not cause to grow. Every kind of fruit and vegetable needed God's warm sunshine and rain to grow. Every kind of animal needed green grass or grain to eat. Green grass and grain need God's sunshine and rain. You will not find one food that did not need God to help it grow. Is that why we should thank Him for food?

A Little Talk about God and You

1. Did you find any food that did not need God to help it grow? Every food needed God's sunshine or rain or creation.
2. Who made you? Can you stay alive long without food? Who made your food? Have you thanked God today for your food? Perhaps you would like to do that now.
3. Have you thanked Mother and Father for buying and cooking food for you? Perhaps you would like to do that now also.

BIBLE READING: Genesis 1:29,30.
BIBLE TRUTH: Give us each day our food for that day. From Luke 11:3.
PRAYER: Thank You, Lord, for food to eat. Thank You for Mother and Father, who help to buy and cook the food that You have made. Amen.

Tall Tales

Brian was telling some friends a tall tale. It just wasn't true. Some friends snickered and said he was fibbing. Some other friends said he was lying.

Brian was trying to make his friends think he did something he did not do. Then his friends would think he was very important. Do you think tall tales work this way?

A Little Talk about Lying

1. What was Brian trying to do? Would you say he was fibbing, telling a tall tale, or lying?
2. Have you heard a friend tell a lie? How did you feel when you heard this? Have you ever told a lie? How do you think other people felt when they heard you? How did you feel?

Brian may think his friends will like him better when he tells his tall tale. But they won't. They will like him less. They will know that he is lying. It's hard to think good things about a person who is lying, isn't it?

That is something for you and me to remember the next time we plan to tell a tall tale.

A Little Talk about Jesus and You

1. Do you think Jesus would ever lie about anything? Why not?
2. Do you think Jesus' friends should ever lie about anything? Why not?
3. What does Jesus think when His friends tell a lie? Do you think He is ashamed of them?

BIBLE READING: Proverbs 6:16-19.
BIBLE TRUTH: The Lord hates lying lips, but loves people who tell the truth. From Proverbs 12:22.
PRAYER: Lord, remind me to tell the truth so that You will never be ashamed of me and so that people can trust me. Amen.

What Have You Planted?

Three farmers plowed their fields and planted their crops. One farmer planted wheat. The second farmer planted corn. The third farmer planted oats.

The crops grew and became ripe. They were ready to be harvested.

Which farmer harvested oats? Which harvested corn? Which harvested wheat?

A Little Talk about Harvesting

1. Do you think the third farmer harvested wheat? Do you think the first farmer harvested corn? Why not?
2. Do we always harvest the kind of crop we plant? Do we ever plant a crop of corn and harvest a crop of wheat? Why not?
3. Do we plant bad things in our lives and harvest good things from them? Why not?

A farmer who plants wheat harvests wheat. That's what the first farmer harvested.

A farmer who plants corn harvests corn. That's what the second farmer harvested.

A farmer who plants oats harvests oats. That's what the third farmer harvested.

A boy or girl who plants dirty or evil thoughts in his or her mind harvests dirty or evil behavior. But a boy or girl who plants what Jesus wants in his or her life harvests behavior that pleases Jesus. Which do you want to harvest?

A Little Talk about Jesus and You

1. What kind of thoughts does Jesus want you to plant in your heart and mind? What kind of thoughts does He not want you to plant there?
2. What would you like to ask Jesus to help you do?

BIBLE READING: Galatians 6:7-10.
BIBLE TRUTH: A person harvests what he sows. From Galatians 6:7.
PRAYER: Teach me to put the right kinds of thoughts in my heart and mind, Lord. Then I will have words and deeds come out of my heart and mind that please You. Amen.

Someone with Me

Jeff looked as sour as a green apple when he came home from school.

"Bad day?" asked Mother.

"I wanted to walk home through the park," said Jeff, "but not one of my friends would come that way with me. I had to walk home alone."

"But you weren't alone," said Mother. "I know someone was with you."

Jeff looked puzzled. "Who?" he asked.

A Little Talk about Someone with You

1. What did Mother mean? Who do you think walked through the park with Jeff?
2. Do you feel sad when all your friends want to do something else? Do you ever feel that no one is with you?
3. What do you think Mother will tell Jeff?

"Someone special promised that He would always be with you," said Mother. "He will always be with you, even when nobody else is."

"Wow, that's quite a friend!" said Jeff.

"Jesus is quite a friend," said Mother. "No other friend has promised that. Right?"

"Right," said Jeff. "I think I'm going to my room and thank Him for going through the park with me today."

A Little Talk about Jesus and You

1. Who are some of your best friends? Do even your best friends make you feel sad sometimes?
2. Mother told Jeff about a friend who would never hurt him or make him feel sad. This friend will be with you at all times. Who is He?
3. Would you like to thank Jesus for being with you at all times? Would you like to thank Him now?

BIBLE READING: Hebrews 13:5,6.
BIBLE TRUTH: Jesus is always with you. From Matthew 28:20.
PRAYER: Thank You, Jesus, for being with me all the time. And thank You for being with me everywhere. Amen.

Larry's Worry

Larry was worried about the special trip his family was taking. They had never been to the Rocky Mountains before. He wanted to be sure everything worked out right.

First Larry worried about leaving puppy in the kennel. Then he worried that he might forget his camera. And then he worried that he might get lost.

A Little Talk about Worrying

1. Pretend you are Father or Mother. You are on this trip with Larry. What would you say to him about worrying?
2. What do you think Jesus would say about worrying? Can you think of some good Bible verses that would help Larry?

"We have time to learn some Bible verses on this trip," said Father. "Here are some verses that will help you stop worrying, Larry."

1. "Trust in the Lord with all your heart" (Proverbs 3:5).
2. "Commit your way to the Lord" (Psalm 37:5).

Father is saying these from his Bible. Be sure to learn them in the Bible translation you use.

A Little Talk about Jesus and You

1. Do you believe Jesus can take care of you? Do you trust Him to do it?
2. "Commit" means to give something to Jesus for safekeeping. Will you give your next hour, or day, or week, or trip to Jesus and let Him guide you?

BIBLE READING: Proverbs 3:5,6.
BIBLE TRUTH: Trust God completely and He will guide you. From Proverbs 3:5,6.
PRAYER: Help me trust You in all ways, and every day, for I know You will guide me in the right path. Amen.

How Much Can You Forgive?

Two men did something wrong. One man stole five dollars from a friend. Then he was sorry for what he had done and asked his friend to forgive him.

The second man killed a little boy. While he was in prison someone told him about Jesus. The man accepted Jesus as his Savior and became a strong Christian leader. He was very sorry that he had killed the little boy and begged the boy's parents to forgive him.

A Little Talk about Forgiveness

1. What did the first man do that was wrong? Was that as bad as killing a little boy? Do you think the friend forgave this man for stealing his money?
2. What did the second man do that was wrong? Was this worse than stealing five dollars? Do you think the parents forgave this man for killing their little boy? Would you forgive him if you were one of these parents?

When the first man asked his friend to forgive him, he gave him back the five dollars. He said he was sorry. But his friend was not a Christian. He did not know much about forgiveness. He had never asked Jesus to forgive him. So he said he would not forgive his friend.

When the second man asked the boy's parents to forgive him, he could not give the boy back to his parents. He could never do that. But the parents were Christians. They loved their boy very much. But they also loved Jesus very much. They had asked Jesus to forgive their sins, and they knew He had. So they forgave the man. They even gave the man a Bible to read and said they would pray for him.

A Little Talk about Jesus and You

1. Why did the first man refuse to forgive his friend? Why did the parents forgive the boy's murderer? What was the difference?
2. Have you asked Jesus to forgive your sins? Do you think He has? Has anyone asked you to forgive him for something he has done? What should you do?

BIBLE READING: Mark 11:25.
BIBLE TRUTH: Forgive our sins as we forgive others who sin against us. From Luke 11:4.
PRAYER: Dear Jesus, You have forgiven me. Teach me to forgive others too. Amen.

FORGIVEN

Right Now!

Rick was so hot and thirsty! He had been playing ball in the backyard with his friends for an hour. Rick ran into the kitchen where Mother was mixing bread dough. Rick wanted some lemonade in a big pitcher in the refrigerator, but he couldn't reach it.

"May I have some lemonade?" Rick asked Mother.

"I'll get it for you as soon as I finish mixing the bread dough," said Mother. "I have dough on my hands now."

"But I'm thirsty!" said Rick. "Can't you get it for me right now?"

A Little Talk about Patience

1. What did Rick want? When did he want it?
2. Why couldn't Mother get the lemonade for Rick right now? How did Rick feel about that?
3. Have you ever thought you couldn't wait for a drink of water? But you could, couldn't you? We can each be patient and wait a little longer for something we want, can't we?

"I will be happy to get the lemonade for you in about three minutes," said Mother. "You can wait that long, can't you? While you are waiting, why don't you watch how I mix the bread dough?"

There was nothing else to do, so Rick watched Mother mix the dough. He had never watched her do this before. It was fun to see what Mother was doing. It was fun to hear her tell how she made fresh bread. Rick thought how much fun it would be to eat the fresh bread with strawberry jam later.

Before long Mother was through. She wiped the bread dough from her hands and went to the refrigerator. Then she poured two glasses of lemonade, one for Rick and one for herself.

"Thank you, Mother," said Rick. "I guess I did learn to be more patient today. And do you know what? This lemonade actually tastes better because I waited for it."

A Little Talk about God and You

1. What did Rick learn? Would he have learned patience if Mother had given him the lemonade as soon as he asked for it?
2. Does God give us everything we want as soon as we ask for it? Why not?

BIBLE READING: 2 Peter 1:5-9.
BIBLE TRUTH: Put on patience, like clothing. From Colossians 3:12.
PRAYER: Lord, Show me how to be patient and wait for You to do things Your way, and in Your time. Amen.

A Light for My Path

"Oh, it's so dark!" said Tony. "I'm glad you have a flashlight."

"What if we didn't have a flashlight?" Father asked Tony. "Let's turn it out and see what it would be like."

When Father turned off the flashlight, Tony could not see the path that went back to their campground. He could not see anything around him. Tony was glad when Father turned the flashlight on again. He could see the path clearly now.

"The world without Jesus would be like this place without a flashlight," said Father. "Do you know what that means?"

A Little Talk about Light

1. Have you ever been on a path on a dark night? Were you glad to have a flashlight? Why?
2. What does a flashlight do? How would you find your way on a dark path without a flashlight?

"Jesus said that He is the light of the world," said Father. "Can you think of some ways He brings light to our world today?"

"He shows us the way to heaven," said Tony.

"He also shows us the right way to live here on earth," said Father. "What if all churches disappeared tomorrow morning, and all ministers and Sunday school teachers, and all Bibles and Christian books? What if all Christians stopped being Christians? What kind of a world would this be?"

"Wow, it would be a mean and dark world!" said Tony. "I'm glad Jesus gives us His light!"

A Little Talk about Jesus and You

1. What difference would it make if there were no Bibles on earth? What difference would it make if there were no churches or preachers or Sunday school teachers? How do you think things would change?
2. How would your family be different if no one had ever heard of Jesus? How would you be different?

BIBLE READING: John 1:1-9.
BIBLE TRUTH: Jesus said, "I am the light of the world. Whoever follows me will not walk in darkness." From John 8:12.
PRAYER: Thank You, Jesus, for bringing light to our dark world. And thank You for shining light on the path to guide me everyday. Amen.

What to Do with a Messy Room

Have you ever had a messy room? Most boys and girls do at one time or another. But when Mother went into Dawn's room today she saw an **extra**-messy room. Dawn's toys were not picked up, her clothes were thrown on a chair, and her bed was not made. What would you say if you were Dawn's mother?

A Little Talk about Keeping Clean

1. Is your room usually clean or usually messy?
2. Do you like to have a clean room? How do you get a clean room? Who must keep it clean?

Dawn's mother didn't say anything. She went downstairs quietly. Dawn wondered why Mother did not scold her.

Later Dawn went downstairs. When she came into the kitchen, she was so surprised. There were pots and pans everywhere. Some were stacked in front of the refrigerator so that Dawn could not get a snack.

Dawn went into the living room to find Mother. But when she got there she was even more surprised. There were books thrown all over the floor, and even some coats. Everywhere Dawn looked, she saw a big mess.

"Mother! Mother!" Dawn said when she saw Mother. "What is wrong with the house?"

"Wrong?" said Mother. "Nothing is wrong, Dawn. It looks just like your room."

Mother was right. The house looked just like her room. Then Dawn was ashamed.

Dawn hurried upstairs. When Mother came to her room a few minutes later, she smiled. Dawn's room was as neat as it could be. And when Dawn came downstairs, the rest of the house was neat too, just the way Mother always kept it.

"Let's keep all our rooms neat from now on," said Dawn.

"Sounds like a good idea to me," said Mother.

A Little Talk about Jesus and You

1. How would you like your house or room to look if Jesus would visit this afternoon? But Jesus is visiting this afternoon, isn't He?
2. Why does Jesus want us to be neat and clean?

BIBLE READING: 1 Corinthians 14:40.
BIBLE TRUTH: Do everything in a neat and orderly way. From 1 Corinthians 14:40.
PRAYER: Dear Jesus, may I never make You ashamed of me or my room or the things I do. Amen.

Are You Wise?

"A friend at school today said I am dumb," Ray complained.

"Let's see about that," said Mother. "Have you told anyone about Jesus this week?"

"Yes," said Ray. "I told this friend about Jesus and he said I am dumb to believe such things."

"That's not what the Bible says," Mother told Ray. "The Bible says that you are wise."

"Where does it say that?" Ray wanted to know.

Do you know?

A Little Talk about Being Wise

1. Has anyone ever called you dumb? Why? Has anyone ever said that you are dumb to believe in Jesus?
2. Why did Ray's friend call him dumb? Do you know why Mother said that Ray is wise? Do you know which Bible verse she is thinking about?

"Here it is," said Mother. "It is Proverbs 11:30."

Then Mother read Proverbs 11:30. This is what it says: "He who wins souls is wise." This means that we are wise if we tell people about Jesus so they can accept Him as their Savior.

Do you know people who are wise? Are you?

A Little Talk about Jesus and You

1. Why do you want your friends to know Jesus? What can He do for them?
2. Do you tell your friends what Jesus can do for them? You are wise if you do.

BIBLE READING: Daniel 12:3.
BIBLE TRUTH: Whoever wins people to Jesus is wise. From Proverbs 11:30.
PRAYER: Dear Jesus, You are my Savior and Friend. I want to win others to You so You will be their Savior and Friend too. Amen.

Forgiving Debts

When Gregg went on a field trip with his class he borrowed a dollar from one of his friends for some ice cream. He borrowed two dollars from another friend for some souvenirs. And he borrowed two dollars from still another friend for a poster. Another friend lent him a dollar for popcorn.

On the way home Gregg began to figure up how much he owed. He could hardly believe it! He owed six dollars to his four friends! How could he ever pay all that money back?

When Gregg got home he looked so worried that Father asked him about it. Then Gregg told Father what had happened. He told Father how sorry he was that he had done this.

A Little Talk about Debts

1. What did Gregg do that was foolish? How do you know he was sorry that he had done this?
2. If you were Gregg's father, what would you say to him now? What would you do?

"I will pay your debts for you this time," said Father. "Just as Jesus paid my debts for me."

$1.00 = $6.00

"Did you borrow too much money from someone?" Gregg asked.

Father smiled. "No, not money," he said. "When we sin, we get into debt. We can never pay for all our sins. But Jesus said that He would pay my debts for me. I was sorry for these debts and asked Him to pay for them, and He did."

Have you asked Jesus to pay your sin debts for you?

A Little Talk about Jesus and You

1. What kind of debts did Father pay for Gregg? What kind of debts did Jesus pay for Father?
2. Have you asked Jesus to forgive you and be your Savior? When you do, He forgives the debts you have because of sin, as He did for Gregg's father.

BIBLE READING: Matthew 6:9-15.
BIBLE TRUTH: Jesus will forgive us, just as we forgive others. From Matthew 6:12.
PRAYER: Dear Jesus, forgive me for the wrong things I have done. Remind me to live for You the way You want me to. Amen.

Put a Sentry on Guard

Tim looked at the picture in his storybook for a long time. He tried to think of himself standing there instead of the tall and handsome sentry in his uniform.

"I would guard the king's castle better than any other sentry," said Tim. "No one would get inside to hurt the king."

Uncle Claude smiled. "I'm sure you would," he said. "A sentry is very important. A king needs a sentry to guard his castle. But you need a sentry even more than a king needs one."

A Little Talk about Watching What We Say

1. What did Tim see in his storybook? Why is a sentry important to a king? What does a sentry do? How does a sentry keep bad things from happening to a king?
2. What do you think Uncle Claude meant when he said that Tim needed a sentry? What does Tim need to guard?

"The Bible tells us that we need a sentry at our mouth," said Uncle Claude. Then Uncle Claude read Psalm 141:3 to Tim. The psalm-writer asked God to put a sentry at his mouth. This sentry would guard what he said. He would help the writer to say the right words and not to say the wrong words.

Would you like God to put a sentry at your mouth?

A Little Talk about God and You

1. Why did the psalm-writer ask God to put a sentry at his mouth? What did he want his sentry to do?
2. Would you like God to be a sentry at your mouth? Would you like Him to help you know what to say and what not to say? Perhaps you would like to ask Him to do this.

BIBLE READING: Psalm 141:1-4.
BIBLE TRUTH: Stand like a sentry at my mouth and guard the words I speak. From Psalm 141:3.
PRAYER: Dear Lord, remind me to say the right things and not say the wrong things. Amen.

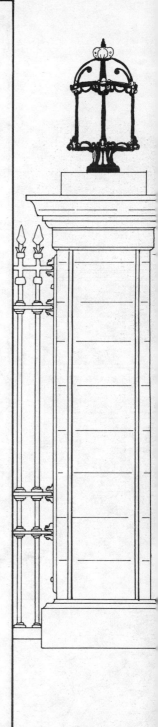

Songs in the Night

Rita was sure that she had never heard such loud thunder before. She was sure that the wind had never blown so loudly before. And she was sure that the rain had never beat so hard against her window before.

It was dark and scary. Rita thought it must be the middle of the night. She jumped from her bed and ran into Mother's and Father's bedroom. Before long she was snug between them.

A Little Talk about Comfort

1. Have you ever been scared because of a bad storm at night? How did you feel? What did you do?
2. How do you think Rita felt? What did she do? What do you think Mother and Father will say to her? Why do you think Rita felt snug and comfortable now?

Rita cuddled close to Mother and Father. Suddenly Mother began to sing to Rita. "Jesus loves you, this I know, for the Bible tells me so," Mother sang. Then Mother sang another song, and another. Before long Rita hardly heard the thunder or saw the lightning. And before long the storm was over.

Father carried a very sleepy Rita back to

her bed and tucked her in. As Rita yawned, she thought she could still hear Mother's songs in the night. She was not afraid now.

A Little Talk about God and You

1. What helped Rita feel comfortable, even during a bad storm? Why do you think Mother sang songs in the night to Rita?
2. The Bible tells us that God gives us songs in the night. Which of these sings to us: the soft night breezes, the sounds of birds, or the gentle patter of rain on our roof? Can you think of other songs in the night that God sends to us?

BIBLE READING: Job 35:10,11.
BIBLE TRUTH: God sings songs in the night to us. From Job 35:10.
PRAYER: Dear God, when I am afraid, please sing songs in the night to me. And thank You when Mother or Father remembers to do that too. Amen.

You Don't Love Me!

"You don't love me!" Liz shouted when Father had to spank her. Liz had become angry at the dinner table and had thrown some of her food on the floor. That's when Mother scolded Liz and Liz said some sassy things to Mother. And that is when Father spanked her.

And that is when Liz shouted "You don't love me!" Father was quiet for a moment before he answered. "I spanked you because I **do** love you," he said. Who do you think is right, Liz or Father?

A Little Talk about Love

1. Why do you think Liz said that Father didn't love her? Have you ever felt that way when Mother or Father had to discipline you?
2. What if parents never spanked or disciplined their children? How would children learn what they should do or shouldn't do?

"Liz, do you really think that we should throw food on the floor?" Father asked. Liz looked on the floor at the mess she had made. She knew that someone would have to clean it up. She was sure that Mother and Father would make her do it.

"If you were a mother, would you let your little girl say sassy things to you?" Father asked.

Liz looked at Mother. Mother looked sad now. Liz and Mother always had fun together. Liz didn't want to make Mother sad. She was sure that what she had done was wrong.

Liz ran over to Mother. She threw her arms around Mother and said she was sorry. Then she threw her arms around Father and told him she was sorry. Then she got some paper towels and mopped up the mess on the floor.

A Little Talk about Jesus and You

1. Do you think Mother and Father were glad that Liz said she was sorry? Why? Is Jesus glad when we tell Him we are sorry for bad things we do? Why?
2. Is Jesus glad when we do what is right? Is He sorry when we do what is wrong? How do we learn what is right and what is wrong?

BIBLE READING: Hebrews 12:5-11.
BIBLE TRUTH: The Lord disciplines those He loves. From Hebrews 12:6. We respect fathers who discipline us. From Hebrews 12:9.
PRAYER: Lord, when You discipline me, I will remember that You are doing it to show me what is right. And I will also remember this when my parents discipline me. Amen.

Something Better than Gold

Dwight stared at the beautiful gold plates and vases in the museum. "Wow, are those really pure gold?" he asked.

"That's what it says here," said Uncle Elmer. "That big vase there is worth more than your house."

Dwight stared at the vase even more now. It was hard for him to think that one vase could be worth more than his house. But that's what Uncle Elmer had said.

"Gold must be worth more than anything else in the world," said Dwight.

Uncle Elmer thought for a moment. "No, you have something in your room that is worth much more," he said. "Do you know what it is?"

A Little Talk about What's Worth Most

1. Have you ever seen pure gold? Have you seen a pure gold dish or vase worth more than your house?
2. What do you think Dwight has that is worth more than gold?

Dwight thought a long time. "I can't think of anything except my family," he said. "You are worth more than gold to me."

Uncle Elmer smiled. "Thanks, Dwight," he said. "But we are not in your room. Let me tell you what it says in Psalm 19:10. It says that God's Word, the Bible, is more precious than gold and sweeter than honey. Do you know why?"

Dwight listened and waited for Uncle Elmer to say why. "First, God gave us His Word, so it's a special gift from a very special Person," said Uncle Elmer. "Then He gave us His Word to help us learn how to live with Him forever. That's special too. Gold can't measure up to either of those."

"Then I should read it more often," said Dwight. And that's what he did.

A Little Talk about God and You

1. What did Dwight have that is more precious than gold? Why is it worth so much?
2. What does Dwight plan to do with God's Word? Would you like to read it more, or have someone read it to you more? What do you think you will learn in God's Word?

BIBLE READING: Psalm 19:7-10.
BIBLE TRUTH: God's Word is more precious than gold and sweeter than honey. From Psalm 19:10.
PRAYER: Thank You, dear Lord, for giving me Your Word that is worth more than gold. Remind me to remember to read it each day and learn more about You. Amen.

If I Were God

"If I were God I wouldn't make any rain," said Damon. Of course Damon and his parents were sorry to see the rain come and spoil their picnic. They had just spread out a blanket and put the food on it. Now they would have to go home.

"Would you really stop making rain if you were God?" Father asked on the way home.

"Yes," said Damon. "Then it wouldn't spoil picnics anymore."

"A lot of other things would stop too," said Father. "Can you name some of them?"

A Little Talk about God's Ways

1. Has the rain ever spoiled your picnic or something you were going to do? Did you ever ask God to stop sending rain?
2. Can you name some things that would stop if there were no more rain? Do you think Damon's idea is good or bad? Why?

Damon began to think. He thought of the flowers in the backyard that would not grow. He thought of the green grass that would turn brown. And he thought of all the trees and bushes that would not get water.

"What about the cows that could not give milk anymore because they would have nothing to eat?" Father asked. "We would have no more meat to eat because every animal must eat something that needs rain. Fish would die because the streams would dry up. And the place where we have our picnic would not be a beautiful forest anymore. It would be dead and dry."

Damon thought for a moment. "I guess God does know what He is doing," he said. "I would just mess up His good plans."

A Little Talk about God and You

1. Do you think Damon's ways are better than God's ways? Why not?
2. Do you think you could do a better job than God? Why not? God's ways of doing things are exactly right, aren't they? So let's thank Him for the way He does things, even though a little rain or snow may bother us at times.

BIBLE READING: Psalm 25:8-10.
BIBLE TRUTH: The Lord's ways are loving and faithful. From Psalm 25:10.
PRAYER: Thank You, dear God, for doing everything right. Keep me from thinking I could do anything better than You. Amen.

Mercy

One day two men were brought before a king. The first man was a very wicked man. He had killed another man who had done nothing wrong. The king could see that this man was not sorry for what he had done. He might kill another man.

"Put that man in prison," said the king. People called that "justice" because the king gave the man what he deserved.

The second man was not a wicked man. He had killed another man but it was an accident. He was very sorry for what had happened and begged the king not to put him in prison too. What do you think the king will do?

A Little Talk about Mercy

1. What had the first man done? What had the second man done? How was the second man different from the first man?
2. What would you do if you were the king? Why? What do you think the king will do? Why?

The king felt sorry for this man. He knew the man did not want to hurt anyone.

"I will set you free," said the king. "I forgive you. You will not go to prison."

The man bowed down and thanked the king. He knew the king could have sent him to prison. But he didn't. The king felt sorry for the man and forgave him, even though he could have punished him. When someone does that, it is called "mercy."

Has someone shown mercy to you? That's when someone gives you something you don't deserve. Or someone doesn't punish you when you deserve it.

A Little Talk about Jesus and You

1. Have you ever done anything wrong? Every one of us has done something wrong, haven't we? That is called sin. We deserve to be punished for our sin, don't we?
2. How do you think Jesus feels when we are proud and are not sorry for our sin? Does He forgive us then? How do you think He feels when we are sorry for our sin and ask Him to forgive us? Does He forgive us then? Jesus wants to show mercy to us, just like the king did.

BIBLE READING: Psalm 103:1-14.
BIBLE TRUTH: Praise the Lord, for He heard me cry for mercy. From Psalm 28:6.
PRAYER: Thank You, dear Jesus, for showing mercy when You could have punished me. I'm so glad that You love me. Amen.

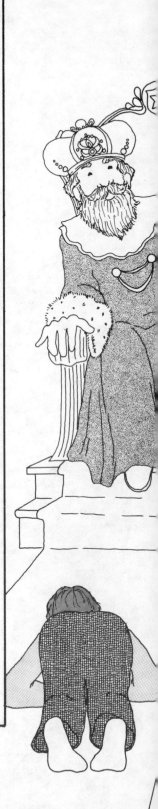

Does God Take Care of Me?

A shepherd once had many sheep. He hired some men to help him take care of them.

Each night the shepherd and his men took turns watching the sheep. They kept the wolves from killing the sheep.

One night a helper fell asleep when he should have been watching. The wolves came and killed many of the sheep. What would you say to this helper if you were the shepherd?

A Little Talk about Taking Care of Someone

1. What did the helper do that was wrong? What should he have done? What happened because of this?
2. Has Mother or Father asked you to watch a little brother or sister for a while? Or have they asked you to take care of something? Did you do a good job?

Did you know that God watches over you day and night? He never goes to sleep, even when you do. He stays awake all the time to take care of you.

What would you like to say to Him for doing this?

A Little Talk about God and You

1. Will God ever fall asleep when He should be watching over you? Why not? How does that make you feel about God's care for you?
2. Would you like to thank Him for taking care of you so well? Why not do that now?

BIBLE READING: Psalm 121:1-8.
BIBLE TRUTH: The Lord, who watches over you, will never go to sleep. From Psalm 121:3,4.
PRAYER: Thank You, dear Lord, for watching over me day and night. Help me to be faithful when I am asked to watch over someone else. Amen.

Do You Remember to Pray?

"It's time to pray before you go to bed," Mother said to Jack. But Jack wanted to finish reading one more page in his book. Then he wanted to get some things ready for school the next day. And then he wanted to clean up his room a little. After that Jack said he should feed his goldfish.

Jack did a lot of other last-minute things too. At last Mother said, "Not one more thing. It's bedtime and that's that." Sometimes mothers have to say those kinds of things, don't they?

But Jack was so tired now that he couldn't pray. He fell asleep before he finished.

Would you like to talk to Jack about praying? What would you say?

A Little Talk about Praying

1. Did Jack put prayer first or last? What happened to keep him from praying as he should?
2. Why should we pray each day? How would you feel if your mother or father would not talk to you today? How does Jesus feel if you do not talk to Him all day?

Mother and Jack had a little talk about prayer when Jack got home from school the next day. "Let's make a list of the things you must do this evening," said Mother.

Jack made a list. There were six things Jack had to do. He was sure to put on the list things like feeding his goldfish.

"In front of each one let's put a time when you plan to do it," said Mother.

Jack smiled. He wrote "before dinner" in front of things like "feed goldfish" and "clean up room." Then he put a special time to read the Bible and pray just before bedtime. Do you think this is a good idea?

A Little Talk about Jesus and You

1. Should we set aside a special time to read our Bible and pray? Why?
2. Do you think that Jesus will forget about you today? If He doesn't forget us, we should not forget Him, should we?

BIBLE READING: Psalm 86:1-7.
BIBLE TRUTH: Have mercy on me, O Lord, for I pray to you all day long. From Psalm 86:3.
PRAYER: Listen while I pray, dear Jesus, for I want to talk to You often through the day. Amen.

Do You Like to Obey?

"Sit!" Cindy said to her dog Lance. But Lance looked up with sleepy eyes and rolled over.

"Mother," said Cindy, "Lance will not obey me. He should be ashamed of himself."

"This reminds me of dinnertime last night," said Mother with a smile. "I called and called, but a girl named Cindy did not come."

Cindy looked down at the floor. "I'm sorry," she said. "It is important to obey, isn't it?"

A Little Talk about Obeying

1. What did Lance do that Cindy did not like? Why?
2. What had Cindy done that was like Lance? What do you think Mother should tell Cindy about this?

"Why do you want Lance to obey you?" asked Mother.

Cindy thought for a minute. "What if I knew something is about to hurt Lance? He could get hurt if he does not obey me," said Cindy.

"Any other reason?" Mother asked.

"What if I had something good for him,

like a bone?" said Cindy. "If he doesn't obey me when I call, he won't get it."

"Those are two good reasons," said Mother. "And they are two good reasons for boys and girls to obey their parents, and Jesus."

"I promise that I will try to obey you and Jesus from now on," said Cindy. "And I'm glad Lance didn't obey today so we could have this little talk."

A Little Talk about Jesus and You

1. What did Cindy learn about obeying? What are two good reasons to obey parents and Jesus?
2. Jesus gave another reason for obeying. Look at the Bible truth below.

BIBLE READING: John 14:23,24.
BIBLE TRUTH: Jesus said, "If you love me, obey what I say." From John 14:15.
PRAYER: Jesus, I'm glad that I can talk with You and be Your friend. I'm glad that I can obey You, because I know that You will always help me do what is right. Amen.

LITTLE TALK 44

Two Friends

Chelsea had two friends, Kitty and Karen. When Chelsea got into trouble one day, Kitty pretended that she did not even know her. But Karen did everything she could to help Chelsea get out of trouble.

Which friend was a true friend?

A Little Talk about Friends

1. Who were Chelsea's two friends? Which one stayed with her when she got into trouble? Which one did not?
2. Have you ever heard of a "fair-weather friend"? That's a friend who is a friend only when things are going well. Which of Chelsea's friends was a fair-weather friend?
3. Which kind of friend is a true friend? Which kind of friend do you want? Which kind of friend do you want to be?

"A friend loves at all times," Father read that night in the Bible.

"What verse is that?" Chelsea asked.

"Proverbs 17:17," said Father. Then Chelsea told Father and Mother about her two friends.

Father and Mother prayed with Chelsea. They asked Chelsea to be a true friend when one of her friends got into trouble. Are you a true friend too?

A Little Talk about Jesus and You

1. Think of some true friends. Who are they? Did you remember your mother and father? Did you remember Jesus?
2. Jesus said, "I will be with you always" (Matthew 28:20). Can you ask anyone to be a better friend than that?

BIBLE READING: Matthew 28:20.
BIBLE TRUTH: A friend will love you all the time. A brother will stick with you even in times of trouble. From Proverbs 17:17.
PRAYER: Thank You, Jesus, for being a true friend. Teach me to be Your true friend, and a true friend to other people too. Amen.

Don't Quit Now

"I quit!" said Bruce.

Uncle Lyle stopped reading and looked at Bruce. "You just started," he said.

"But I don't like this book," Bruce answered. "I don't know why the teacher told us to read it."

"You'll never get the field plowed that way," said Uncle Lyle.

Bruce looked puzzled. "What do you mean?" he asked.

A Little Talk about Quitting

1. When was the last time you quit doing something that you should have kept on doing?
2. Why did you quit?
3. Do you think it is wrong to get in the habit of quitting? Why?

"One day Jesus talked about following Him," Uncle Lyle told Bruce. "He said it is like plowing."

"How is following Jesus like plowing?" Bruce asked, looking puzzled.

Uncle Lyle smiled. "When I was a boy, I lived on a farm," he said. "When a farmer plows the first row across the field, he must keep looking at one tree or post. That's the way he plows a straight line. If he looks back, he will begin to plow a crooked line."

"So if I keep looking back and wanting to quit, I will not do well in my reading?" asked Bruce.

"That's right," said Uncle Lyle. "When you start doing something worth doing, keep looking ahead until it's done. That's what Jesus was saying."

"Well, I guess I had better start plowing again," Bruce said with a laugh.

A Little Talk about Jesus and You

1. What was Jesus saying about quitting? What happens when you keep looking back instead of looking ahead?
2. Is there something you should do, but you don't like to do it? What do you think Jesus wants you to do to get it done?

BIBLE READING: Luke 9:62.
BIBLE TRUTH: Someone who starts a good work must keep looking ahead until it is done. From Luke 9:62.
PRAYER: Dear Jesus, may I do what You want me to do. Thank You for helping me get it done. Amen.

Harvesting the Crops

Long ago, before modern farm machines, a farmer had a wonderful crop of wheat. It was the best crop he had ever had. But he could not find people to help him cut it and tie it into bundles. He could not find people to help him thresh it.

The farmer worked hard. He worked many hours. But he could not harvest all his wheat before winter came. The winter rains and snow broke the wheat stalks. Some of it went into the mud and was lost. Some rotted in the fields.

The farmer was sad. He had a wonderful crop. All he needed were helpers. Do you know how this farmer is like Jesus?

A Little Talk about Harvesting

1. What kind of a crop did this farmer have? Why couldn't he get it all harvested?
2. How do you think this farmer is like Jesus?

Jesus said that there is a big crop of people who want to know Him as their

Savior. They are like the big field of grain. There are many thousands of them, all over the world. These people need to hear what Jesus has done for us. They need to hear us tell what Jesus can do for them.

But there are not enough people going out to help these people come to Jesus. Jesus is like this farmer. He has a wonderful crop. He wants to harvest it. But He wants us to help Him harvest it.

We have much work to do for Jesus, don't we?

A Little Talk about Jesus and You

1. How would you feel if you were the farmer? What would you think if you could not get all your wheat harvested?
2. How would you feel if you were Jesus? What would you think if you did not have enough helpers to tell other people how to get to heaven?
3. What can you do for Jesus now?

BIBLE READING: Matthew 9:35-38.
BIBLE TRUTH: There is a wonderful harvest of people who want to know Jesus. But there are not enough workers to tell them about Him. From Matthew 9:37.
PRAYER: Dear Jesus, give me the courage to tell my friends about You. Then I will be one of the helpers You want. Amen.

A Crown for You

Jeremy and Uncle Steve were reading a favorite storybook about kings and queens.

"But why do kings wear those strange hats?" asked Jeremy.

"Those are crowns," said Uncle Steve. "They are often made of gold and have lots of jewels. A crown would be worth as much as your house, and maybe more."

"But why would a king want to wear it?" said Jeremy. "It doesn't look as soft and warm as my cap."

"A crown tells us that the person wearing it is a king or a queen," said Uncle Steve. "But did you know that someday you will wear a better crown than a king or queen can wear?"

A Little Talk about Crowns

1. Why do kings and queens wear crowns? What do the crowns tell us?
2. What do you think Uncle Steve meant when he said that someday Jeremy could wear a crown?

Jeremy looked puzzled. "But how could I become a king or queen?" he asked. "And where would I get enough money to buy a gold crown and lots of jewels?"

Uncle Steve smiled. "You can have a much better crown that that," he said. "It can be a crown worth so much that no one could buy it."

"Wow! How do I get it?" asked Jeremy.

"The Bible calls it a crown of righteousness," said Uncle Steve. "Paul said he was getting one for doing Jesus' work and living for Jesus as he should. That's how we can get one of these beautiful crowns from Jesus too."

A Little Talk about Jesus and You

1. What kind of crown was Uncle Steve talking about? How did he say that people get it?
2. What do you think Jesus wants you to do for Him? Will you?

BIBLE READING: 2 Timothy 4:7,8.
BIBLE TRUTH: Jesus wants us to follow Him and do His work. He has a special reward for us when we do. From Revelation 2:10.
PRAYER: Dear Jesus, I want to follow You and do Your work each day. Thank You for Your promise of a beautiful crown. Amen.

Growing

"Look how you have grown since last year!" the doctor told John. John and his mother smiled as they looked at the place where the doctor measured boys and girls.

John was still smiling when he and Mother came home. "I'm going to get as big as that doorway," said John. "Maybe bigger! Then I can play football or basketball, or I can wrestle the biggest guys on TV."

"You can grow even bigger than that," said Mother. "But you can do it without being an inch taller or a pound heavier."

John looked surprised. "How can I do that?" he asked.

A Little Talk about Growing

1. How was John growing? How do you measure the way John is growing?
2. What do you think Mother will say to John? Can you think of ways you grow that cannot be measured by inches and pounds?

"The Bible tells us how Jesus was growing when He was 12 years old," said Mother.

"How tall was He?" John asked. "How much did He weigh?"

"It doesn't tell us either of those things," said Mother. "But it tells us something more important about the way Jesus was growing."

Mother opened her Bible and read Luke 2:52. Do you know what it says? Would you like to read it now?

A Little Talk about Jesus and You

1. After you have read Luke 2:52, name four ways Jesus was growing at age 12.
2. Check your list with this one: 1) He grew wiser, knowing more and using what He knew better; 2) He grew bigger and taller and stronger; 3) each day He did more things that pleased God; and 4) each day He did more things that helped other people.

Hang this list on your wall. Look at it each evening to see if you are growing that way.

BIBLE READING: Luke 2:51,52.
BIBLE TRUTH: Jesus grew wiser, and bigger, and helped God and other people more each day. That is the way God wants us to grow too. From Luke 2:52.
PRAYER: Dear Jesus, help me grow the way You did. I want to be more like You. Thank You for living in my heart. Amen.

MY GROWTH CHART
wiser
bigger
helpful
kind
loving

Helping a Sick Friend

"Nancy is sick today," Priscilla told her mother. "I feel so sorry for her. I wish I could help her."

"You can," said Mother. "Would you like to know how?"

A Little Talk about Helping a Sick Friend

1. Has a friend of yours been sick this week? What did you do to help your friend?
2. What do you think Mother told Priscilla about helping a sick friend? Think of some ways you can help when your friend is sick. Talk with your mother or father about this.

"Have you prayed for Nancy today?" Mother asked Priscilla. "It's always good to ask Jesus to help a sick friend."

"Will He make my sick friend well if I ask Him?" Priscilla asked.

"Sometimes He will," said Mother. "But you can also ask Jesus to take care of your sick friend while she is sick."

"I will do that now," said Priscilla. "But what else could I do for Nancy?"

"You could call her mother and ask if Nancy is well enough to talk with you on the phone," said Mother. "And you could ask her mother if you may bring something for Nancy. Perhaps you would like to make a fun gift for her. You could give it to her mother to give to Nancy."

Priscilla ran to her room. She had three important things to do for her friend Nancy.

A Little Talk about Jesus and You

1. What three important things will Priscilla do for Nancy? Why will these please Jesus?
2. Have you been sick lately? What would you like a friend to do for you when you are sick?

BIBLE READING: Mark 2:1-12.
BIBLE TRUTH: We can ask Jesus to help a sick friend. From Mark 2:3.
PRAYER: Dear Jesus, please help my sick friend now. May this friend know that You are there and will do good things even though he or she is sick. Amen.

Will the Plants Grow?

Duane thought it was fun to help Mother and Father plant seeds in the garden. The soil was soft and Duane let it run through his fingers. Duane opened a package of seeds. On the package were pictures of red beets. He put the hard, crinkly seeds in the little furrow that Father had made.

Then Duane opened another package. This had pictures of carrots on it. He sprinkled those seeds in another furrow.

When Duane had finished, Mother raked soft dirt over the furrows with a hoe. It was so much fun to plant the garden together!

Then Duane looked worried. "What if they won't grow?" he asked.

A Little Talk about Seasons

1. What season of the year do we plant gardens? Why don't we plant in the winter?
2. What would you say to Duane about seeds deciding not to grow? Who gave us our seasons and set up the way for seeds to grow?

"God gave us the seasons in the beginning," said Father. "He gave us the springtime to plant seeds. He gave us the warm soft ground where we may plant the seeds. If we plant them God's way, they will grow God's way."

Duane smiled. "I guess they wouldn't grow if we planted them in the winter, would they?"

"Or if we planted them on a rock," said Mother. "Or if we planted them where they would not feel the warm sun or get the rain that God sends."

"God promised that seeds will grow and give us something to harvest," said Father. "But we must plant them the way He said."

"I'm glad we can believe God's promise," said Duane. "Now I will watch each day for the little plants to come up."

A Little Talk about God and You

1. If you want seeds to grow, how must you plant them? Will they grow if you don't plant them God's way?
2. How do you know that seeds will grow if you plant them God's way? Can you trust God to keep His promises? Will He keep other promises He has made to you?

BIBLE READING: Genesis 8:20-22.
BIBLE TRUTH: As long as the earth is here, there will be a time to plant seeds and harvest crops. Cold and heat, summer and winter, day and night will never go away. From Genesis 8:22.
PRAYER: Thank You, dear God, for spring, summer, fall, and winter. Amen.

Is Cheating Worth It?

Dean scratched his head and rubbed his nose. But he just couldn't remember the answer. Then he looked at Faith. She had already written her answer, and it was sure to be right. Faith was always right on things like this. All Dean had to do was move just a little closer and peek over Faith's shoulder.

Dean started to look. Then something inside him nudged him back. He started to look again. But he did not feel good about it.

A Little Talk about Cheating

1. Why do you think Dean is not sure about cheating? Why doesn't he just go ahead and do it?
2. How do you think Dean will feel the next day if he cheats on this test? How would you feel?

"I won't do it," said Dean. "I will feel terrible if I do. And I know that Jesus will not be pleased."

So Dean put down the best answer he could. When he did, it seemed like it should be the right one.

"Even if it isn't the right answer, I've done the right thing," Dean thought.

Do you think Dean did the right thing?

A Little Talk about Jesus and You

1. Do you think Jesus would have been pleased if Dean had cheated? Why not?
2. Do you think Jesus is pleased with the way Dean did this? Why? What would you like to say to Dean now?

BIBLE READING: Philippians 4:8,9.
BIBLE TRUTH: Think about things that are true, great, right, pure, and lovely. From Philippians 4:8.
PRAYER: Dear Jesus, teach me not to cheat, for I know that I will be cheating myself most of all. Amen.

My Warm, Wonderful House

The snow had begun in the middle of the afternoon. By the time Don got out of school it was coming down as if a big pillow had broken in the sky. The wind was howling down the street, blowing the snow into drifts. Don caught his breath as he headed home. The snow blew into his face, and the wind pulled at his cap and coat.

Although each street took him closer to home, he thought he would never get through the wind and snow. Also, it was starting to get dark.

At last Don saw the warm yellow light coming from the window of his house. He could see Mother working inside. He could see smoke coming from the fireplace chimney. Don thought it would be the most wonderful time of the day when he walked into his house.

A Little Talk about Being Thankful

1. Have you ever walked through a bad snowstorm? How did it feel? How did you feel when you saw your house at last?
2. What do you think Don will say when he walks into his house? What would you say?

"I'm home! I'm home!" Don shouted as he walked into his house.

Don had never before thought that his house was so wonderful. There was Mother, smiling at him. The house was filled with the wonderful smells of dinner, and a fire was crackling in the fireplace. Most wonderful of all, this was his home.

A Little Talk about Jesus and You

1. Are you thankful for your home? If you are, thank your parents for it tonight. Also thank Jesus. He helped your parents get your home.
2. Do you suppose this is the way it will feel when we get home in heaven? Living in this world is sometimes like walking through a big snowstorm. How wonderful it will be to be home with Jesus!

BIBLE READING: Psalm 127:1.
BIBLE TRUTH: The Lord blesses the home of a godly person. From Proverbs 3:33.
PRAYER: Thank You, dear Jesus, for a warm, wonderful home, and for my family who lives there. Amen.

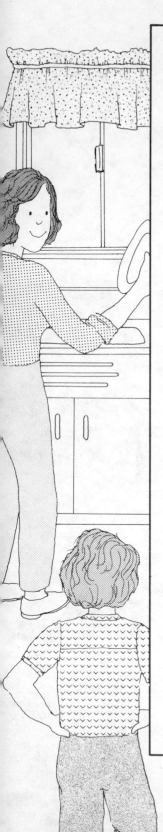

Do You Like to Wash Dishes?

"I don't want to help wash the dishes!" Megan shouted. "It's no fun to wash dishes and I won't do it!"

Mother smiled at Megan. "All right, why don't you just run out and play?" she said.

That night Megan sat down at the dinner table. She was hungry and ready to eat one of Mother's good dinners. Then she looked at her plate. It was dirty, just the way she had left it after breakfast. It had egg and jelly all over it. It still had a little piece of leftover toast.

A Little Talk about Being Clean

1. How would you like to eat dinner on a dirty breakfast dish? Why not?
2. Why is it important to wash dishes after we use them? Why is it important to wash our hands, our clothes, our towels, our sheets, and our pillowcases? Why wash your car or scrub your floor or vacuum your carpet?

"Shall I put your dinner on your plate, Megan?" Mother asked.

"No, thank you," said Megan. "May I wash my plate first?"

"But I thought you didn't want to wash dishes," said Mother.

"I'll never say that again!" said Megan. "I don't want to eat dinner on dirty dishes, so I'll be glad to help you wash them from now on."

Do you think Megan will ever complain about washing dishes again?

A Little Talk about Jesus and You

1. The Bible tells us that Jesus will wash our sin away. He will make us clean. Read 1 John 1:9.
2. Why did Megan want to wash her dirty plate? How does our dirty plate remind you of sin in our lives? Why do you want Jesus to wash your sin away?
3. Have you asked Jesus to do this? If not, would you like to do it now?

BIBLE READING: Psalm 51:1,2.
BIBLE TRUTH: If we tell God about our dirty sins, and ask Him to wash them away, He will make us clean. From 1 John 1:9.
PRAYER: Dear Jesus, thank You for dying for my sins. Wash them away and make my heart clean. Amen.

Walking Together

Anita slammed the door and threw down her schoolbooks. Mother had never seen her come home from school so angry before.

"After you close the door quietly and pick up your books, let's have some cookies and milk," said Mother. "We can talk about it then."

"Talk about what?" Anita asked.

"What's bothering you," said Mother.

Anita became more cheerful when she sat down with Mother. Cookies and milk with Mother always took the grumpiness away.

"It's Gwen," Anita began. "We're supposed to decorate our room at school for the party. But what I want doesn't matter. Gwen won't listen to me."

Mother was quiet for a long time. "Do you listen to Gwen?" Mother asked.

Now Anita was quiet. "But. . .but why doesn't she listen to me?" Anita asked.

A Little Talk about Listening

1. Have you ever thought someone was not listening to you? Were you listening to that person?
2. What would you tell Anita if you were Mother?

"Do you remember the street in front of

the bakery downtown?" Mother asked. "Do the cars all go one way, or two?"

"One way," said Anita.

"Suppose a car started down the street one way," said Mother. "Then another car started up the street, the other way?"

"They would crash in the middle," said Anita.

"Like you and Gwen," said Mother. "You are both trying to go the opposite way. You keep crashing in the middle."

Anita smiled now. "You are right, Mother," she said. "May I go over to Gwen's house now? We can talk about going in the same direction."

A Little Talk about Jesus and You

1. Does Jesus want us to keep having trouble with friends, like Anita and Gwen? Or does He want us and our friends to do things together?
2. Are you and a friend "crashing into" each other like Anita and Gwen? Will you ask Jesus to help you work together?

BIBLE READING: Amos 3:3.
BIBLE TRUTH: Two people do not walk together unless they both want to do it. From Amos 3:3.
PRAYER: Dear Jesus, it's no fun to keep crashing into my friends. I want to learn to walk with them and not against them. Amen.

Wonderful Things

Barry had never been at Niagara Falls before. He had never seen so much water in one place. And he had never heard such a roaring noise from water.

Suddenly Barry saw a beautiful rainbow appear near the falls. "Look!" he shouted. "It's wonderful!"

Mother and Father both smiled. "It really is wonderful," said Father. "We never get tired of seeing and hearing this wonderful place."

It was a bright summer afternoon, with deep blue sky and billowy white clouds. Barry and his family walked through the beautiful gardens on the Canadian side of the falls. Everything seemed filled with color.

At last the soft colors of the evening sunset began to paint the puffy clouds. Barry did not know where to look next. He kept looking from the falls to the flowers. Then he looked from the sky to the falls.

"I can't think of a word for it all," said Barry.

"I can," said Father. "Want to know what it is?"

A Little Talk about Wonderful Things

1. Have you ever been to a place where everything seemed beautiful? Where was it? What did you like most about it?

2. Can you think of the word that Barry wants?

"What is the word?" Barry asked.

"Majesty!" said Father. "It means something very wonderful, very great, above all that we usually know. It's a good word to tell us about God's wonderful works."

"I like that word," said Barry. "It sounds like the wonderful things we have seen. It is a good word for God's wonderful works."

"It's also a good word to tell us about God," said Father. "God is a wonderful God, and has done wonderful things for us. All He is and does and says is majesty."

A Little Talk about God and You

1. Aren't you glad that a God who does such wonderful things loves you? Aren't you glad that He takes care of you each day?
2. Do you like the word "majesty"? The next time you think about God, remember that word. You will remember how wonderful God is. You will also remember what wonderful things He has given us.

BIBLE READING: Psalm 29:1-11.
BIBLE TRUTH: The voice of the Lord is full of majesty. From Psalm 29:4.
PRAYER: Thank You, Lord, for wonderful things. And thank You for Your majesty. Amen.

My Coat

"I don't need to wear my coat outside today," Glen argued.

Glen ran outside and began to play ball. But a strong wind blew and he began to shiver. Soon Glen ran into the house and put on his coat. Mother smiled as she watched him.

"It's much colder out there than I thought," said Glen. "I'm glad for my warm coat."

A Little Talk about My Clothing

1. Have you ever run outside without a coat but found that it was too cold? What did you do?
2. What did Glen do? Why did he say that he was glad for his warm coat? What would you like to say to Glen about his coat?

"We should all be glad for warm coats and for all our other clothing," said Mother. "Do you know where we get it?"

"At the store, I suppose," said Glen.

"But where does the store get it?" asked Mother.

Glen thought awhile. "Someone makes it from cloth and stuff," he said.

"And where do we get the cloth and stuff?" asked Mother.

Glen thought longer. But he wasn't sure about that.

"Some cloth comes from cotton plants," said Mother. "God sends the sunshine and rain to make the plants grow. Wool comes from sheep who eat the green grass that God grows. Everything we have comes from God. Even things like nylon and rayon come from gifts that God gave us."

"So God gave my coat to me," said Glen. "I'm glad He did! It will keep me warm while I play outside today."

A Little Talk about God and You

1. Every piece of clothing you have has come from God. Even the "man-made" cloth is made from something that God made.
2. Have you ever thanked your parents for your clothing? Have you ever thanked God for it?

BIBLE READING: Matthew 6:28-34.
BIBLE TRUTH: God will give you good clothes to wear. From Matthew 6:30.
PRAYER: Thank You, God, for my clothes. I would be cold and ashamed without them. Amen.

How Loyal are You?

Ben thought it was fun to sleep in his pup tent in the backyard. He made sure to take his flashlight and sleeping bag. And he asked Towser to guard the tent.

Twice during the night Ben shined his flashlight out of the tent. Each time he saw Towser, lying next to the tent flap. In the morning, when Ben woke up, Towser was still there. He wagged his tail when Ben came out of the tent.

"There must be a good word for a dog like you," said Ben.

A Little Talk about Loyalty

1. What does loyal mean? Was Towser loyal? Why did he stay by the tent flap all night?
2. Can you think of ways you can be loyal?

"Towser is loyal," said Father when Ben told him what happened. "You can always count on someone who is loyal."

"Sometimes my friends seem like friends, and sometimes they try to hurt me," said Ben. "That's not being loyal, is it?"

"Some friends are loyal," said Father. "They never try to hurt you."

Ben smiled. "I guess you and Mother are that kind of friends," he said. "You always try to help me and never try to hurt me."

A Little Talk about Jesus and You

1. Is Jesus a loyal friend? Will He ever try to hurt you? Will He always try to help you?
2. What kind of friend are you to Jesus? Are you always loyal to Him? What kind of friend should you be to Jesus?

BIBLE READING: Ruth 1:16-18.
BIBLE TRUTH: A loyal friend is a friend at all times. From Proverbs 17:17.
PRAYER: Dear Jesus, I want to be loyal to You always, just as You are my faithful friend at all times. Amen.

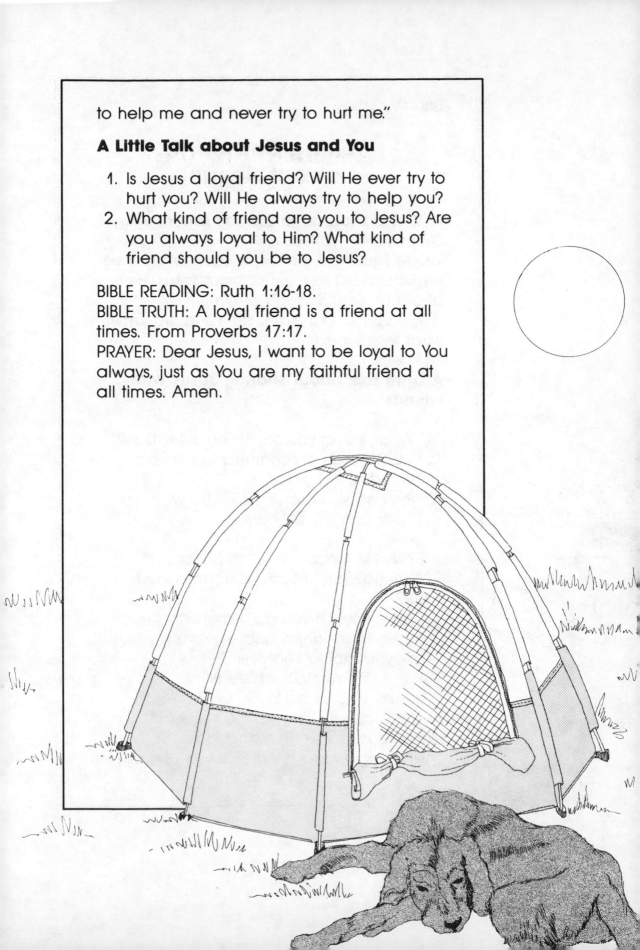

Telling Someone about Jesus

"Why do you go to Sunday school every Sunday?" Bill asked.

Dan squirmed. He didn't know what to say. He was afraid to tell Bill about Jesus. He was afraid Bill would laugh at him.

"I. . .uh. . ." Dan said, but he didn't know what to say next.

A Little Talk about Sharing Jesus with Friends

1. What would you say if you were Dan? Would you be ashamed to tell your friend about Jesus?
2. Pretend you are Dan. Tell Bill what you think Dan will tell him.

"I have a friend there," said Dan.

"A friend?" Bill asked. "Is it someone I know?"

"I don't know if you do," said Dan. "But since He is my friend and you are my friend, I think you should know Him."

"What's his name?" asked Bill.

"Jesus," said Dan. "If you will come to Sunday school with me, you will learn about Him and become His friend too."

Bill thought for a minute or two. "Since you

and Jesus are such good friends, and you and I are such good friends, I'll come next Sunday," said Bill.

A Little Talk about Jesus and You

1. Is Jesus your special friend? Is someone else your special friend too? Would you like your other special friend to be a friend of Jesus?
2. What did Dan do to help Bill become a special friend of Jesus? What can you do to help one of your special friends know Jesus?

BIBLE READING: John 1:35-42.
BIBLE TRUTH: Andrew brought his brother Simon to Jesus. You can do that too. From John 1:41,42.
PRAYER: Dear Jesus, thank You for being my special friend. Teach me to bring some other special friend to You. Then that person and You can be good friends too. Amen.

Learning by Being Quiet

"Andrew, what you did was not right," said Mother. "May I tell you what you should have done?"

Andrew began to make excuses. Some of his excuses really became arguments. Every time Mother tried to tell him what he had done wrong, Andrew made an excuse or argued. Every time she tried to tell him what he should have done, Andrew made another excuse or argued. What would you say to Andrew?

A Little Talk about Listening

1. Do you know anyone who argues or makes excuses when Mother or Father talks to him or her?
2. What would you say to Andrew right now? What would you tell him about listening?
3. Can you listen and learn while you are arguing or making excuses? Why not?

"If you won't listen to me, will you listen to Job?" Mother asked Andrew.

Andrew looked surprised. "Who?" he asked.

"Job," said Mother. "A book of the Bible is named for him. God was trying to teach Job some things. Do you think Job argued or made excuses?"

Andrew shook his head "No." Then Mother read this from Job 6:24: "Teach me, and I will be quiet; show me where I have been wrong."

"Does that mean children should be quiet and listen when parents are trying to teach them something?" Andrew asked.   Mother nodded her head "Yes." You should do that too, shouldn't you?

A Little Talk about God and You

1. Do you think a person should argue with God when God is trying to tell him something? Why not?
2. How does being quiet and listening help us to learn what God wants? How does being quiet and listening help us to learn what our parents want?
3. What would you like to do from now on when your parents or God try to tell you something important? Will you?

BIBLE READING: Job 6:24,25.
BIBLE TRUTH: I will be quiet while You teach me; show me how I have been wrong. From Job 6:24.
PRAYER: Dear God, teach me to be quiet and listen when I want to argue or make excuses. Amen.

Have You Met My Friend Dorcas?

Everyone in church loved Mrs. Welch. Perhaps that is because she was always there to visit sick people and take food to families that needed it.

"She's a Dorcas," Maria's mother told her.

"A what?" asked Maria.

"Have you met my friend Dorcas?" Mother asked. "There's a story about her in the Bible." Then Mother read the story about Dorcas to Maria and asked Maria some questions about helping other people.

A Little Talk about Helping Others

1. Why did everyone in church love Mrs. Welch? Do you know anyone like her?
2. Why is it fun to help others? Would it be more fun to keep everything you have for yourself and never give anything away? Would it be more fun to spend all your time doing things for yourself, but never doing anything for others? Why not?

Would you like to read the story of Dorcas or have someone read it to you? You will find it in Acts 9:36-42.

Get Well

A Little Talk about Jesus and You

1. What kind of person was Dorcas? Why do you think she did so many wonderful things for people? Why did people love her so much?

2. Do you think Jesus is pleased when we are like Dorcas? Why? Would you like to be more giving like Dorcas? What are some things you could do?

BIBLE READING: Acts 9:36-42.
BIBLE TRUTH: Whoever loves God should also love his brother. From 1 John 4:21.
PRAYER: Dear Jesus, You have told me to love others and help those who have a special need. Give me a loving heart and busy hands to do Your work. Amen.

How Do You Know There Is a God?

"How do you know there is a God?" Dave asked the old man down the street. "Some of my friends asked me, and I didn't know what to tell them."

What would you say to Dave if you were the old man?

A Little Talk about God

1. Have you ever asked Dave's question? You can't see God, or hear Him talk, or touch Him, or smell Him. So how do you know He is there?
2. What would you like to say to Dave? Do you have some good answers?

The old man picked up his Bible. "This is a long letter from God to you," he said. "It tells us much about God. We know many things about God by reading this letter."

"But some of my friends don't believe the Bible," said Dave. "What else can I tell them?"

"We live in a wonderful world," said the old man. "It is filled with things that couldn't just happen by accident. Each snowflake is different. Each fingerprint is different. Each sunset is different. Someone had to make these things. When you see a clock, you know there was a clockmaker. When you see a car, you know there was a carmaker."

"So God is a worldmaker?" said Dave.

"Exactly, and that is why we call Him the Creator," said the old man. "It's another way of saying a worldmaker. But it also says that He made the sun, moon, stars, and everything else."

Dave smiled. "You're right," he said. "We can't have a world without a worldmaker, or stars without a starmaker, or a sky without a skymaker."

"Or a Dave without a Davemaker," said the old man with a smile.

A Little Talk about God and You

1. Who wrote the Bible? Who made the world and all that is in it? Who made the sun, moon, and stars? Can you have all these wonderful things without someone to make them?
2. Who made you? Did you know that He made you different from all other people in the world? There is no one exactly like you. Can that "just happen"?

BIBLE READING: Isaiah 40:28-31.
BIBLE TRUTH: God made the heavens and the earth. From Genesis 1:1. God is the One who made us, and we belong to Him. From Psalm 100:3.
PRAYER: Thank You, Lord, for making me and for taking care of me each day. Amen.

Father's Arms

Shopping at the mall was fun for the first hour. It was even a little fun for the next half hour. But now Melanie was so tired that she couldn't walk another step. She even started to cry.

"Oh, dear, it looks like our shopping trip is over," said Mother.

Melanie held up her arms toward Father. "Will you carry me?" she asked.

A Little Talk about Care

1. Why is Melanie so tired? Do you ever get tired when you go shopping for a long time? What does Melanie want Father to do?
2. What do you think Father will do? What would you like to say to Melanie's father right now?

Father smiled and reached down. He

picked Melanie up and cuddled her in his arms. Then Melanie put her head on Father's shoulder as he carried her to their car.

"Feel better now?" asked Mother.

Melanie smiled. "Much better," she said.

A Little Talk about God and You

1. Why did Melanie feel better now? Do you feel better when you are tired and can rest in Father's or Mother's arms?
2. Sometimes when we feel we can't go on, God takes us in His arms. We can't see His arms, but they are there. The Bible says that it is so. Would you like to thank Him for holding us when we think we can't go on?

BIBLE READING: Deuteronomy 33:27.

BIBLE TRUTH: God is like a strong father as He holds us in His arms. From Deuteronomy 33:27.

PRAYER: Thank You, dear God, for holding me when I am tired and can't go on. Amen.

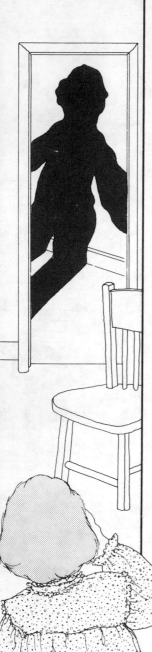

My Voice

Andrea sat up in bed and looked at the soft light in the hallway. She saw a shadow of a person coming toward her door. The shadow looked big and dark. Suddenly Andrea was afraid. She began to cry.

A Little Talk about Being Afraid

1. What did Andrea see? Why is she so afraid?
2. What do you think is making that shadow? What would you like to say to Andrea?

"Don't cry, Andrea," a voice said softly. "It's only me."

Andrea stopped crying as soon as she heard her big sister's voice. Andrea's big sister came into the room. Andrea put her arms around her sister and hugged her tight.

A Little Talk about Jesus and You

1. Are you ever afraid of the shadows of the trees or bushes at night?
2. But you wouldn't be afraid if Jesus whispered softly to you, would you? You wouldn't be afraid if He put His arms around you and hugged you.

BIBLE READING: John 10:14-16.
BIBLE TRUTH: Jesus' friends follow Him because they know His voice. From John 10:4.
PRAYER: Dear Jesus, when I am afraid, please be with me. Then I will not be afraid anymore. Amen.

Can I Hide from God?

"Let's play hide-and-seek," said Emily. "I'll hide and you find me."

Mother smiled as Emily ran around the house. She knew that Emily would hide in her favorite hiding place behind a tree. Mother pretended to look in another place or two. But before long she shouted, "I found you!"

"How did you find me so fast?" asked Emily.

A Little Talk about Hiding

1. How did Mother find Emily so fast? What do you think she said to Emily?
2. Would Mother have found Emily as fast if she had been the girl down the street? Would she have known where to look? Why not?

"I found you because I know you," said Mother. "I know where you like to hide."

"Do you suppose God could find me as fast as you did?" Emily asked.

"Faster," said Mother. "He knows each one of us. He knows what we think and where we try to hide from Him. That's why we can never hide from Him."

And that's why we should never try to hide from Him, isn't it?

A Little Talk about God and You

1. Have you ever tried to hide from God? Have you done something you did not want God to see? Have you hoped He would not see it?
2. Can you ever hide from God? Why not?

BIBLE READING: Psalm 139:1-12.
BIBLE TRUTH: Where can I hide from You? Where can I run away from You? From Psalm 139:7.
PRAYER: I know that I cannot hide from You, dear God. I cannot run away from You, either. So teach me how to do what You want so that I will not want to run or hide. Amen.

How Big Is Jesus?

"Father, how big is Jesus?" Eric asked.

Father put down his newspaper. "Do you mean how tall or how much He weighs?" he asked.

"Not exactly," he said. "But what big things can He do? Is He bigger than Superman?"

Father smiled. "Tell me what Superman can do," he said.

"He can jump over a building and fly faster than an airplane," said Eric. "He can pick up a car and throw it across the street. Can Jesus do those things?"

A Little Talk about Being Big

1. What did Eric ask Father? What did Father ask Eric? What are some different ways to be big?
2. What would you say to Eric? Do you think Jesus is bigger than Superman? Could Jesus do bigger things?

"I have never heard of Jesus jumping over buildings, or flying faster than airplanes, or throwing cars across the street," said Father. "But did Jesus ever need to do any of those things?"

Eric thought about that. He thought of some of the Bible stories he had learned. But he could not think of any time Jesus needed to jump over buildings or throw cars across a street.

"But let's think of some things Jesus did," said Father. "Let's ask if Superman could do them."

Eric smiled as Father began telling some wonderful things that Jesus had done. "He made a blind person see," said Father. "He made a dead girl come back to life. And He made the wind and the stormy waves of the sea be quiet. Could Superman do any of those things?"

Eric gulped. He had never heard of anyone, even Superman, who could bring a dead girl back to life, or make a blind person see, or make the wind and waves obey him.

"Jesus is much bigger than Superman," said Eric. "I'm glad He loves me and wants to help me too."

A Little Talk about Jesus and You

1. Who do you think is bigger, Jesus or Superman? Why?
2. Are you glad that Jesus loves you and wants to help you?

BIBLE READING: Matthew 8:23-27.
BIBLE TRUTH: The winds and the sea obey Him. From Matthew 8:27.
PRAYER: Dear Jesus, I know You can do anything. Even the winds and sea obey You, so help me to obey You too. Amen.

Kioko ♡ Marzine ♡ Lorenzo ♡ Augustine ♡ Eric ♡ Josep
Ginny Buffy ♡ Jennifer ♡ Brian ♡ Lauren ♡ Richard Karen
Tsu Kioto ♡ Calf ♡
Beverly Laurie ♡ Samu
Boris ♡ Ray
♡ Robin ♡ Jeff Erin
Rick Ralph Tory Chas
Lois my Joe
♡ Patty Dad Charle
Toshiko Ken Lynd
♡ Cindy Wet
Schennetta Bill
Lisa Sandy Todd Pat
Huong ♡ Chris Kare
♡ Trevor Nat
Joan ♡ Tito Iar
Bob ♡ Jacque Sally
Heidi Yoland
Sarah ♡ Amy ♡ Be
Fritz Ed ♡ Tim
Shetry June Fran
Pam Robe
Jason ♡ David char ♡ Elizabeth ♡ Roy
Charlotte Jimmy Linda
Corinna Ryan Gil Adelle
♡ Juanita

LITTLE TALK 66

Someone Special Knows My Name

"I feel so alone in my new school," said Alice. "I don't think anyone knows my name yet."

"Oh, yes, one person at your school knows your name," said Mother. "This is the most important person in your school."

Alice looked surprised. "Who?" she asked.

A Little Talk about Your Name

1. Do Mother and Father know your name? Do your special friends know your name? Do strangers know your name?
2. Why are you glad when someone special knows your name? Do you like to hear a special person say your name?

"This is the most special person in the world," said Mother. "He is your best friend."

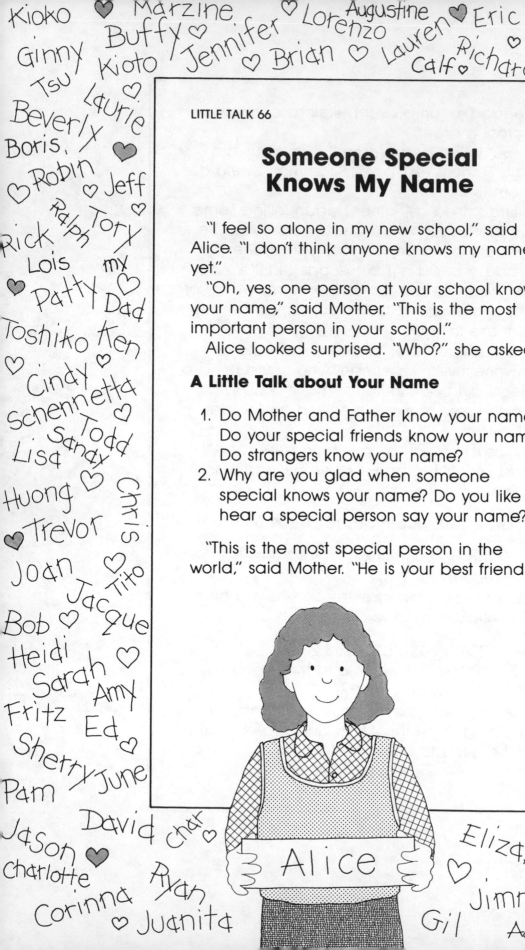

Alice

Alice smiled. "Are you talking about God?" she asked.

"Yes, He says that He knows your name," said Mother. "He has a lot of names to remember, but He will never forget yours."

A Little Talk about God and You

1. If God knows Alice's name, does He know yours too? Will He ever forget your name?
2. Why are you glad that God knows your name? How does that tell you that He loves you?
3. What would you like to say to God now? Will you?

BIBLE READING: Exodus 33:17.
BIBLE TRUTH: I know your name. From Exodus 33:17.
PRAYER: I'm glad, dear God, that You know my name. That tells me that You love me and will not forget to help me each day. Amen.

Grandfather's Lamp

"This lamp belonged to my mother," Grandfather told Donna. "It was the only light we had when I was a little boy. When I read my books at night, this lamp gave me my light."

"Wow!" said Donna. "It's beautiful. May we light it?"

Grandfather lit the old oil lamp. Then he turned out all the lights. Donna read her favorite book in the light of the old lamp.

"What else did you do with the old lamp?" asked Donna.

"When we went into another room, we carried the old lamp with us," said Grandfather. "It showed us where to go in the dark. That's why this old lamp is like the Bible."

"How is that?" asked Donna.

A Little Talk about Lamps and Light

1. Do you like old oil lamps like Grandfather's?
2. How do you think the old oil lamp is like the Bible?

"Did you know that the Bible is a lamp?" Grandfather asked. "It says so in the Psalms."

Donna smiled. "Is that because it shows us where to go?" she asked.

"Yep!" said Grandfather. "That's it. If you read your Bible each day, God will show you where to go. He will guide you through His Word."

Donna was sure that she would keep on reading her Bible each day. And she knew that God would guide her as she did.

A Little Talk about God and You

1. Do you read your Bible each day? Does it help you know what God wants?
2. Don't forget to pray, too. Ask God to guide you each day.

BIBLE READING: 2 Peter 1:19-21.
BIBLE TRUTH: God's Word is a lamp for our feet, and a light for our path. From Psalm 119:105.
PRAYER: Thank You, Lord, for giving me Your Word. Thank You for letting it bring light to each step I take. Amen.

Why Quarrel?

Connie watched her mother and father hug each other. She noticed the warm twinkle in their eyes and the smile they gave each other.

"Why don't you quarrel with each other like Jacque's parents do?" she asked. "Jacque says they are always quarreling and saying mean things to each other."

"Would you rather we do that than hug and kiss?" asked Mother.

A Little Talk about Love

1. What would you say if you were Connie? Do you think Connie's parents love each other? Why do you say that?
2. Is it any fun to quarrel? Why not? Which makes you happier, showing love or quarreling?

"I'd rather have you hug and kiss," said Connie. "Then I know that you love each other. It's much more fun to live in a happy home than a home full of quarreling."

"There are times when each of us disagrees with someone," said Father. "Mother and I do not always agree. But we are always kind to one another. And we always talk until we understand each other."

Then Father and Mother each gave Connie a big hug.

A Little Talk about Jesus and You

1. Would you like Jesus to be mean and to quarrel with you all the time? Why doesn't He?
2. If Jesus is kind and loving with us, how should we be with each other? How should we be to Him?

BIBLE READING: 1 John 2:9-11.
BIBLE TRUTH: We need to love one another, because love comes from God. 1 John 4:7.
PRAYER: Dear Jesus, thank You for Your love. Amen.

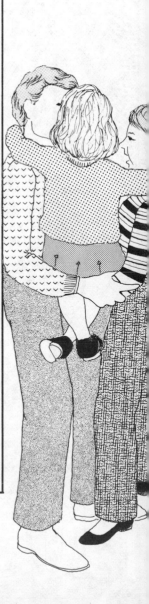

What Is Your Inheritance?

"Did you see that article in today's paper about the hundred-million-dollar inheritance?" Father asked Mother.

"What's an inheritance?" asked Dick.

"It's something a father or mother leaves a child," said Father. "Usually it's money. But it could be other things too."

"Will I get an inheritance from you someday?" asked Dick.

"You probably will not get much money," said Father. "But you will get something worth more than money."

A Little Talk about Inheritance

1. What did Father say an inheritance is?
2. What do you think Father will say? What inheritance could be worth more than money? Can you think of some things you would rather get from your mother and father than money?

"Mother and I are giving you some things that are worth more than money," said Father. "Can you think of some?"

"You've taught me to pray," said Dick. "And you've taught me to love God's Word."

"Those are worth much more than money," said Father. "Anything else?"

"You've helped me want to please Jesus," said Dick. "I want to do the things He wants me to do."

"Mother and I have helped you learn to love Jesus," said Father. "That will be a good inheritance for you. I hope you will help your children have the same things someday."

Dick was sure he would, but it was hard to think about his children. So he thanked Father for the wonderful inheritance and ran out to play.

A Little Talk about Jesus and You

1. What kind of inheritance are Mother and Father giving Dick? Why are these worth more than money?
2. Is Jesus pleased with this kind of inheritance? Why? When you grow up and have children, would you like to give them this kind of inheritance?

BIBLE READING: Colossians 1:12.
BIBLE TRUTH: I have a good inheritance.
From Psalm 16:6.
PRAYER: Thank You, dear Jesus, for all that You have given me. And thank You for parents who give me a good inheritance. Amen.

Don't Call Bad Things Good

Carl looked at the newspaper Father was reading. He knew Father was angry because of the article he had just read.

"Is that man dead?" Carl asked, pointing to the picture in the newspaper.

"Yes, some men shot him," said Father. "They said killing him was good."

"Why?" asked Carl. "Did he try to hurt them?"

"No, he didn't," said Father. "But these men did not like what he believed. What they thought and what he thought was different. So they said it was good to kill him."

A Little Talk about Good and Evil

1. Can something good ever be evil? Can something evil ever be good? Good comes from God and evil comes from the devil. So good can never be evil and evil can never be good.
2. Why did these people call their murder good? Which was it, good or evil? Why?

"If a man steals our car, is that good or evil?" Father asked.

"Evil," said Carl.

"Why?" Father asked.

"Because God said we must not steal," said Carl. "It says so in the Bible."

"What are some other things God says are evil?" Father asked.

Carl thought about lying, cheating, and saying bad things about God. He thought of other things that God said we must not do.

"If we do something evil, then call it good, does that make it good?" Father asked.

"No, of course not," said Carl. "If something is evil, just giving it another name does not change it."

"If we say a tree is really a cow, that will not help the tree give us milk," said Father. "And if we call a tree a car, we can't drive it to church. We can't change cows into trees or trees into cars by changing their names. And we can't make evil good by changing its name."

A Little Talk about God and You

1. Why does God hate evil and love good? Why should Christians hate evil and love good?
2. If we call evil good, is it? Why not?

BIBLE READING: Isaiah 5:20,21.
BIBLE TRUTH: Shame on those who call evil good, or call good evil. From Isaiah 5:20.
PRAYER: Dear God, I never want to make evil sound good by giving it a good name. Amen.

Remember to Say Thank You

George smiled at the ice cream man when he paid him for the two cones.

"This one is for you," the ice cream man said to George's friend Jerry. Then he gave the other cone to George. "And this one is for you."

George watched Jerry lick the cone without saying a word. "You're welcome," said George.

Jerry looked puzzled. "Huh? What do you mean?" he said.

A Little Talk about Thankfulness

1. What did Jerry forget to say? What would you like to say to Jerry?
2. Why should we be thankful for good gifts? Why is it wrong not to say "thank you"?

"You missed a great story at Sunday school last Sunday," George told Jerry.

"What was it?" asked Jerry.

"Ten men with leprosy met Jesus. They asked Him to help them. Jesus felt sorry for them, and do you know what He did for them?" said George. "They were not sick any longer. So what do you think the ten men said?"

"I suppose they said 'Thank you' to Jesus," said Jerry.

"Only one thanked Jesus," said George. "The others just went away."

"That wasn't very nice," said Jerry. "Everyone should remember to say 'thank you.' " Suddenly Jerry stopped licking his ice cream cone. He looked at George. Then he looked at his ice cream cone.

"I. . .I guess I wasn't very nice," said Jerry. "I didn't even say 'thank you.' I'm sorry. Thank you!"

"That's okay," said George. "But your ice cream will taste better now."

Jerry began to lick his ice cream cone again. "Do you know what? It really does taste better!" he said.

A Little Talk about Jesus and You

1. What did Jerry forget to do? Why is that wrong?
2. What story did George tell him? How was Jerry like the nine men who were not thankful?
3. Have you forgotten to say "thank you" this week? If you have, why not say it today? Whatever you're thanking some- one for will seem better.

BIBLE READING: Luke 17:11-17.
BIBLE TRUTH: Give thanks at all times. From 1 Thessalonians 5:18.
PRAYER: Give me a thankful heart, dear Jesus. Amen.

The Door

"Please open the door!" Teri shouted. "I can't get in!"

Mother smiled as she opened the kitchen door and Teri came in, arms loaded with books and lunch box. "I'm sorry, but I must have forgotten to unlock the door when I came home," Mother said. "Locked doors are so unfriendly and open doors are so friendly."

Teri looked at the kitchen door. It was open now. She could run in and out easily. But Mother was right. The same door was so unfriendly a few minutes earlier.

"Our kitchen door is like Jesus," said Mother.

"It is?" said Teri. "How?"

A Little Talk about Doors

1. What if there were no door or window in your house? How would you get in or out?

2. Can you get in or out any better if you have doors and windows, but they are all locked? Why not?

3. Can you get in or out easily if your door is open? Does your door keep strangers out? How do you feel when you can lock your door at night and keep strangers

out? How do you feel when you can unlock your door in the morning so you can go in and out easily?

"Jesus said He is like a door," said Mother. "He is like our door when it is open and lets you come into our house. He is the door that lets us go into heaven."

"I'm glad Jesus is an open door," said Teri.

We should all be glad for that, shouldn't we?

A Little Talk about Jesus and You

1. The Bible tells us that Jesus is the only way to get to heaven. That is why He is like a door. Have you asked Him to help you get to heaven? He will.
2. Do you know of any other way to get to heaven? There is no other way, is there? Aren't you glad that Jesus will be your Savior and Friend? Would you like to thank Him for what He has done?

BIBLE READING: John 10:7-10.
BIBLE TRUTH: Jesus is the door to heaven. From John 10:9.
PRAYER: Thank You, dear Jesus, for showing me how I can know You better in heaven. I want to accept You as my Savior and live with You forever. Amen.

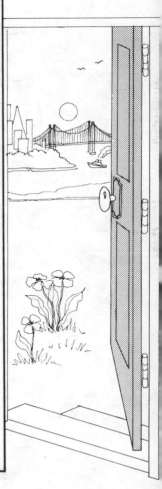

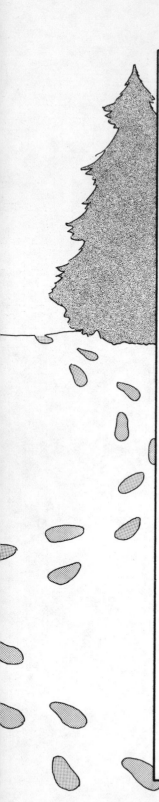

Following the Leader

"Let's play follow-the-leader," said Wesley. "I'll walk in the snow, and you follow my footprints. Then you walk in the snow and I'll follow your footprints."

"That sounds like fun," said Wendy. "Start out and I'll follow as soon as I count to a hundred."

When Wendy counted to a hundred, she followed Wesley's footprints. They went around the house, over the patio, and back to the old shed. Wesley's footprints went to a ladder propped against the old shed. When Wendy looked up, she could see Wesley's footprints on the roof of the shed.

"Wesley! You know that Father said we should not get up on the roof of the shed!" Wendy shouted.

Wendy wanted to play follow-the-leader, but she wanted to obey Father. What should she do?

A Little Talk about Obeying

1. Why didn't Wendy want to go on the shed roof? What would you say to Wendy if you were there?

2. Why was it wrong for Wesley to go on the roof? What would you say to Wesley if you were Wendy?

"I won't go up there!" said Wendy. "You know that Father told us not to do it."

"Aw, come on," said Wesley. "He probably wouldn't care if we came here for a game."

"I'll play follow-the-leader as long as we don't disobey Father or Mother," said Wendy. "And that's that."

Wesley grumbled a little, but he wanted to play follow-the-leader. So before long Wesley and Wendy had many footprints to follow. And they all went where they should.

A Little Talk about Jesus and You

1. What kind of people does Jesus want His people to follow?
2. What do you think Jesus meant when He said we should follow Him? How do we follow Jesus?

BIBLE READING: Matthew 4:18-20.
BIBLE TRUTH: Jesus said, "Follow me." From Matthew 4:19.
PRAYER: Dear Jesus, I want to go where You want me to go and do what You want me to do. Show me what You want me to do. Amen.

Do We Have to Work?

"I hate work!" Diane shouted. "I don't want to do my chores. I don't want to help with the dishes or clean my room. I don't ever want to work again."

Do you think Diane is right?

A Little Talk about Work

1. Have you ever felt like Diane? Have you ever wanted to stop doing chores or helping with the family work?
2. What would you say to Diane? Do you think she is right or wrong? Why?

Mother looked at Father. Father looked at Mother. "Do you suppose we could stop working too?" Mother asked.

"I suppose we could," said Father. "But if you wouldn't make breakfast, lunch, or dinner for us, we could get hungry."

"And if you didn't go to work, we would have no money to buy food," said Mother.

"What would happen if you stopped washing our clothes or cleaning our house or keeping clean sheets on our beds?" Father asked. "It wouldn't be much fun to live in this house if everything was dirty or messed up."

"That's true," said Mother. "Of course if you stopped earning money we would have to sell our house and our car. So we would not have a place to live or a car to take us places."

"Yes, and since you don't plan to work, you would not get a job either," said Father. "So I guess we would have no home, no car, no food, no clothes, no pets, no anything!"

"Stop! Stop!" said Diane. "I don't want to give up all those things. I want to help you with them."

A Little Talk about God and You

1. Will God give us a house and car and clothes and food unless we work for them? Why not?
2. Is it fair for some of the family to work and others not to work? Is it fair for you to do nothing to keep the house clean when Mother and Father do so much?
3. What kind of work can you do to help Mother or Father at home? Will you? Do you think this will please God?

BIBLE READING: Psalm 90:16,17.
BIBLE TRUTH: You will eat when you work. From Psalm 128:2.
PRAYER: I thank You, Lord, for all Your gifts. I thank You for letting me work and do my part to get them and take care of them. Amen.

Someone to Take Care of Us

"What a wonderful mother she will make!" Ed said. He was so happy to see his pet collie with her puppies. While they slept, she lay nearby, watching them all the time.

"Will she ever let them out of her sight?" asked Ed.

"Probably not," said Mother. "She will watch them all the time until they can take care of themselves. Even at night, the slightest whimper will wake her."

"Is that the way God watches over us?" asked Ed.

A Little Talk about God's Care

1. Has your pet ever had babies? How well did she watch over them?
2. Where do you think pets get their loving care? Do you think God gave it to them?

"God does an even better job," said Mother. "He watches over all His people all the time. The Bible says that He never sleeps."

"Is He watching over us right now?" Ed asked.

"Yes, He is," said Mother. "Nothing happens to you that He does not know."

A Little Talk about God and You

1. When does God watch over you? Does He take care of you?
2. Have you ever thanked Him for watching over you and taking care of you?

BIBLE READING: Psalm 121:2-5.
BIBLE TRUTH: The Lord never sleeps. He is always watching over you. From Psalm 121:4,5.
PRAYER: Thank You, dear God, for watching over me. Keep me from doing anything that You would not want to see. Amen.

Pumpkin Faces

It was that time of year when fathers carve pumpkin faces. Peter and Holly were excited when Father lined up three pumpkins to carve faces. The first face was sad. Peter and Holly looked sad as Father carved that face. The next face was scary. Peter and Holly looked afraid as Father carved that one. The last face was smiling. And guess what Peter and Holly did while Father carved that face?

"Looks like we have two pumpkin mirrors here," said Father. Peter and Holly looked puzzled. What did Father mean?

A Little Talk about Faces

1. What do you think Father meant by "pumpkin mirrors"? How did Peter's and Holly's faces look like the pumpkin faces?
2. When you smile, do other people around you smile? When you frown, do others frown? Which do you like to do more?

Father smiled at Peter and Holly. They both smiled back. Then Father slowly let a frown come on his face. They began to frown.

"It works almost every time," said Father. "Faces are like mirrors. They reflect a smile, or a frown, or a scary look."

"Were we reflecting each pumpkin face as you cut it?" asked Peter.

"Yes," said Father, "just like you reflected my smile or frown. If someone is grumpy, try smiling. It may melt the grumpiness away. If someone is sad, try smiling. It may melt the sadness away."

Do you think Peter and Holly smiled a little more after that?

A Little Talk about Jesus and You

1. Why does Jesus want us to have a happy face? Would a sad face show that we are happy to be Christians?
2. Would you like your face to become more like Jesus each day? Would you like your face to show other people that Jesus lives in you?

BIBLE READING: Psalm 4:6,7.
BIBLE TRUTH: Our faces reflect the Lord's glory, and we become more like Him. From 2 Corinthians 3:18.
PRAYER: When I look in the mirror, may I see a smile because You are smiling through me. Amen.

Clean Cups

Elsie was glad that she could help Mother wash the dinner dishes. It was fun to help Mother.

"I'll wash and you dry," Elsie said.

Mother did not care which she did. She was just glad to have Elsie helping her.

Suddenly Mother noticed that the dish towel had brown smudges on it. Then she looked at the cup she was drying.

"Oh, oh," said Mother. "You washed the outside of this cup, but you forgot to wash the inside. Look at this."

A Little Talk about Being Clean

1. Do you help Mother wash dishes? Do you wash only the outside of the dirty cups? Would you like to drink your milk from a cup filled with brown coffee stains? Why not?
2. What do you think Mother will say to Elsie?

"Which is more important to keep clean?" Mother asked. "The inside of the cup or the outside?"

Elsie looked at the cup with the brown smudges on the inside. "The inside," said Elsie. "I wouldn't want to drink milk from that dirty cup."

"Which is more important for us to keep clean?" Mother asked. "Our hands or our hearts?"

Elsie thought about that. "Our hearts," she said. "I think that's what Jesus would want."

A Little Talk about Jesus and You

1. Why do you think Jesus is more interested in a clean heart than clean hands? Does that mean we should not wash our hands?
2. How do we get our hearts clean? Have you ever asked Jesus to clean your heart? If not, would you like to do it now?

BIBLE READING: Matthew 23:25,26.
BIBLE TRUTH: Create in me a clean heart, O Lord. From Psalm 51:10.
PRAYER: Dear Jesus, please take the sin from my heart and make me clean. Amen.

A Parade of Good Things

"Parades are such fun!" said Sandy. "It's so exciting to see each new thing come along!"

"How would you like to watch a parade every day?" asked Aunt Clara.

"How could I do that?" asked Sandy. "We don't have a parade every day."

"Yes, we do," said Aunt Clara. "It's a very special parade, too. Would you like to know what it is?"

A Little Talk about Good Things

1. Do you like to watch a parade? What do you find exciting about it?
2. What kind of parade do you like best? Do you like to watch animals or fire engines? Do you like floats better than marching bands?
3. What do you suppose Aunt Clara means when she says Sandy sees a special parade each day?

"One day God told Moses about this parade," Aunt Clara said. "He told Moses that He would cause all His goodness to pass in front of him. God sends this same parade to us. Each good thing God says or does marches in front of us like it is in a special parade."

"Wow, what a parade!" said Sandy. "God does a lot of wonderful things for us. There must be a long line of His good things."

"There is," said Aunt Clara. "Let's think about some of them."

A Little Talk about God and You

1. Think of five good things that God has done for you this week. Pretend they are marching in a parade in front of you. These may be special gifts, special things He has helped you do, or His special Word that you have read or heard.
2. Now thank God for each good thing as it passes by in front of you. This is a good parade, isn't it?

BIBLE READING: Matthew 7:7-11.
BIBLE TRUTH: I will send all my good things in front of you like a parade. From Exodus 33:19.
PRAYER: Thank You, dear God, for each good gift You send, each good word You speak, and each good thing You do for me. Amen.

How Should We Give?

Two boys gave their mother birthday gifts. One boy spent all his money and bought his mother a beautiful gift, but he played with his friends all day. The other boy didn't have any money, but he made a birthday card for his mother. On the card he told her what a wonderful mother she was and how much he loved her. Then he spent most of the day helping his mother, doing things that she liked to do.

A Little Talk about Giving

1. Which gift was better? Which gift do you like better?
2. Do the best gifts cost the most money? What kind of gifts are best?
3. Will you remember this the next time your mother or father has a special day?

The best gifts are not things. Almost anyone can buy things and give them away. The best gifts are yourself and your love. Nobody else can give that.

What if the gifts were from Mother or Father? Would you rather have some expensive thing without them, or something much less expensive with them? Would you rather have your parents be with you on your birthday or give you something expensive and not be with you?

A Little Talk about Jesus and You

1. What would you rather have from Jesus, His love or lots of money?
2. Jesus said He is with us always. Would you rather have that or a castle without Him?
3. Jesus said that we can live with Him in heaven. Would you rather have that or else be king over a big country? Why?

BIBLE READING: Matthew 6:31-34.
BIBLE TRUTH: It is better to have a little and love the Lord than to have much with a messed-up life. From Proverbs 15:16.
PRAYER: Dear Jesus, give me Your best gifts—Your love, Your home in heaven, and You by my side until I go there to live. Amen.

God's House

"Do I have to go to Sunday school this morning?" Beth complained.

Father put his arm around Beth. "Let me tell you something about our church and Sunday school," he said. "Perhaps then you will want to go."

A Little Talk about Church and Sunday School

1. What do you like best about your church and Sunday school?
2. Why is Beth complaining? What do you think Father will say to her?

"What do you like about our church and Sunday school?" Father asked.

Beth thought awhile. "I like our beautiful building," she said. "It is the prettiest church building in town."

"I like our church building too," said Father. "What else do you like?"

"Everyone is friendly," said Beth. "We have lots of fun in Sunday school. Last Sunday we had some Bible quizzes and I got the most right."

"That does sound like fun," said Father. "What about the songs you sing? Do you like them?"

"Oh, yes," said Beth. "We have lots of fun

singing. And when our teacher prays it seems that God is in the room with us."

"What would you think if someone took our church away?" said Father. "Would you miss it?"

Beth frowned. "I don't like to think about that," she said.

"What if you stopped going? Would anyone miss you?" Beth gave a long list of friends who would miss her.

"Time to go," Mother called from the next room.

"Let's hurry!" said Beth. "We don't want to be late!"

"But I thought you didn't want to go today," said Father.

"I do now!" said Beth.

A Little Talk about Jesus and You

1. What did Beth like about her church and Sunday school?
2. What do you like best about your church and Sunday school?
3. Do you ever thank Jesus for church and Sunday school? Would you like to do that now?

BIBLE READING: Psalm 122:1.
BIBLE TRUTH: I am glad when someone says it is time to go to God's house. From Psalm 122:1.
PRAYER: Dear Jesus, I love to go to Your house because I learn about You there. Amen.

Shhhh!

"Shhhh! Listen!" said Aunt Bess.

"Shhhh! Listen!" said Uncle Earl.

"What do you hear?" asked Lucy.

"That depends," said Aunt Bess. "Listen carefully."

"Be as quiet as you can," said Uncle Earl. "Then tell us what you hear."

Lucy sat on a log with Aunt Bess and Uncle Earl. They looked around the beautiful woods where they were hiking. What do you think they will hear?

A Little Talk about Listening

1. Have you ever hiked in the woods with someone you love? What are some of the sounds that you heard?
2. What do you think Lucy will hear if she is quiet?

Suddenly Lucy heard RAT-A-TAT-TAT-TAT! "I see it!" said Lucy. "That woodpecker is working to make a hole in that big tree!"

BIRK-BIRK-BIRK! said a squirrel on a limb above Lucy. CHI-CHI-CHI! said a bluejay. Then a puff of wind made the leaves above them sigh softly. A bird began to sing sweetly in another tree. Before long, Lucy could count eight different sounds in the woods.

"It's fun to listen," she said.

"It's fun to listen to God's world," said Uncle Earl. "But it's more fun to listen to God. He talks to us through His Word."

Lucy was glad that she could have this listening time. She would listen in other places, too.

A Little Talk about God and You

1. Do you like to listen to your parents? If you do, you will learn many wonderful things.
2. Who else should you listen to? How about your Sunday school teacher, your pastor, and your teacher at school? Can you think of others?
3. When you read your Bible, do you ask God to tell you what He wants you to hear?

BIBLE READING: Isaiah 55:1-3.
BIBLE TRUTH: Listen to me! From Isaiah 55:2.
PRAYER: Lord, tell me what You want me to know in Your Word. Please do this, for I am listening. Amen.

Did You Forget Something?

"I forgot," said Wanda. "I just can't remember the Bible verse we learned last Sunday."

"I'll help you learn it again," said Grandmother. "But first I want to read another verse from the Bible." Grandmother read this part of Proverbs 4:5: "Do not forget my words or swerve from them."

"I didn't know there was a verse like that," said Wanda. "Is God scolding me because I forgot my memory verse?"

A Little Talk about Remembering God's Word

1. Do you ever forget a Bible memory verse? It's easy, isn't it?
2. What do you think Proverbs 4:5 is saying? Is God scolding people who forget memory verses? Or is He saying something else?

"All of us forget memory verses," said Grandma. "It's hard to remember them all unless we keep learning them again."

"Then what is God saying in this verse?" asked Wanda.

"He is talking about people who turn aside from His Word because they want to," said Grandma. "He calls it swerving, like a car swerving off the road. If you do that, you can get hurt. And if you swerve from God's Word, you can also get hurt."

A Little Talk about God and You

1. How does a person swerve, or turn, from God's Word? When a person turns from God's Word, will he also turn from God?
2. Why does God want you to read from His Word each day? Why does He want you to memorize Bible verses? Why does He want you to obey His Word? What will this keep you from doing?

BIBLE READING: Proverbs 4:2-5.
BIBLE TRUTH: Do not forget my words or turn from them. From Proverbs 4:5.
PRAYER: I love Your Word, dear God. Amen.

Smiling Pennies

Casey was dressed up and ready to go to Sunday school. He poured out ten pennies from his bank and counted them. Mother smiled as she watched. But then she looked sad as she saw Casey put one of the pennies back into his bank. Suddenly he put another penny back, and then another.

A Little Talk about Giving

1. The Bible says that God loves a cheerful giver. Do you think God wants Casey's three pennies if Casey doesn't really want to give them? Why not?
2. What do you think Mother will say to Casey? What do you think Casey will say to Mother?

"God loves a cheerful giver," said Mother. Casey frowned and poured the three pennies from his bank. Now he had ten pennies in his hands again. But he had a gloomy frown on his face.

"Have you looked in the mirror?" Mother asked Casey. When Casey looked in the mirror he saw a frowning face.

"Every penny you give has a frown just like yours," said Mother. "Frowning pennies don't please God. Why don't you put them all back in your bank?"

Casey slowly put all ten pennies back into his bank. Then he started to leave his room with Mother. But he felt very sad. He knew he would not be happy if he gave nothing to God.

Suddenly Casey ran back into his room. He poured some pennies into his hand. When he came back to Mother he had a big smile on his face. Then Casey opened his hand and there were 15 pennies in it.

Mother looked at Casey and then at his 15 pennies. "Every penny has a smile on it," said Mother. "God will certainly love this cheerful giver this morning."

A Little Talk about God and You

1. Why did the first pennies have a frown on them? Why did the 15 pennies have a smile on them?
2. If you really don't want to give something to God, does He want it? Why not? Why should we want to give our money to God? What will God and His friends do with it?

BIBLE READING: 2 Corinthians 9:6-8.
BIBLE TRUTH: God wants us to give cheerfully. From 2 Corinthians 9:7.
PRAYER: Dear Lord, I want to give good things to You because I love You. Amen.

Don't Burst Your Balloon

Kent was bragging to his friends. Father heard everything he said.

"I can run faster than anyone in my class," said Kent. "I probably can run faster than anyone in my school. Who knows, maybe I can run faster than anyone in town." Kent didn't stop bragging there either.

When Kent's friends left, Father came into the family room with Kent. "I heard what you told your friends," said Father. "I kept thinking of one word each time you told them how fast you are."

A Little Talk about Bragging

1. Do you like to hear a friend brag? Why?
2. Have you bragged about anything this week? Do you think your friends like to hear you brag? Why not?

"Tell me exactly what you told your friends," Father said to Kent.

Kent's face became red. "Aw, don't make me do that," he said.

"Please go ahead," said Father. "I want you to see something." Kent saw then that Father had a balloon. It had not been blown up yet. What would Father do with it?

Kent said he could run faster than anyone

in his class. Father took the balloon and blew a big puff of air into it.

"Go on," said Father.

Then Kent said he could run faster than anyone in his school. Father blew another big puff of air into the balloon. When Kent said he could run faster than anyone in town Father blew another puff of air into the balloon.

Suddenly the balloon burst with a loud bang. Kent almost jumped out of his chair.

"Three puffs of bragging and the balloon burst," said Father. "I wonder how many more times you could have bragged before you would have burst with pride."

"I won't do it again," said Kent. "I'm sorry."

A Little Talk about Jesus and You

1. How is bragging like blowing up a balloon? How many puffs of bragging did it take to blow up the balloon that Father had?
2. What would you say to Kent about bragging? What will you remember the next time you think about bragging?

BIBLE READING: Luke 14:8-11.
BIBLE TRUTH: Whoever makes himself look big will be made to look little. From Luke 14:11.
PRAYER: Please remind me of that balloon, dear Lord. Keep me from blowing up my pride. I know You would not be pleased. Amen.

Will You Feed a Starving Person?

"I'm glad we don't have to feed those starving people," said Judy.

Mother looked at the magazine that Judy had. There were pictures of dozens of starving people in Africa. Some of them looked so thin and hungry.

"But we do have to feed them," said Mother. "At least we must help to feed them."

A Little Talk about Helping Others

1. When someone is starving, do we have to help feed that person? Why? Why can't we just let that person starve?
2. What would you want other people to do if you were starving? Would you be glad if someone helped you?

"Father and I give money to a group that helps to feed these hungry people," said Mother. "We think that is what Jesus wants us to do."

"Would Jesus help to feed these people if He were here?" Judy asked.

"Yes, I know He would," said Mother. "Do you remember how He fed 5000 hungry people one day?"

Judy remembered that story from Sunday school.

"May I give part of my dinner tonight to these people?" Judy asked.

"We have no way to send your dinner to Africa," said Mother. "But if you want to give some of your money, we can help you do that."

So that's what Judy did. Perhaps you would like to do that too.

A Little Talk about Jesus and You

1. How many people did Jesus feed one day? Read Luke 9:10-17.
2. Why would Jesus want you to help feed starving people? Why would He want you to help them in other ways too?

BIBLE READING: Matthew 25:31-40.
BIBLE TRUTH: Since God loved us so much, we must also love one another. From 1 John 4:11.
PRAYER: Dear Jesus, You loved me enough to die for me. Let me love You enough to live for You. Amen.

What Started the Forest Fire?

"What a terrible forest fire!" Father said. He put the newspaper down. "And they found that it started with one person who was careless after he lit a match."

Julie looked at Father's newspaper. There was a picture of a house burning. It looked like their house.

"Did that house burn in the forest fire?" she asked.

"More than 50 houses burned in that fire," said Father. "It shows what one careless person can do. But your tongue or mine can start a worse fire than that one match."

"How?" asked Julie.

A Little Talk about What We Say

1. Have you ever seen a big fire? What did you think of it? Do you think it did a lot of damage?
2. What did Father mean when he said that your tongue or mine could cause an even worse fire?
3. Are you ever careless with what you say? Have you ever hurt someone by saying something careless? Has anyone ever hurt you by saying something careless?

CLOSE BEFORE STRIKING

"The Bible says that our tongue can start a fire by what we say," Father told Julie. "It says it is even like a forest fire."

"Does the Bible really say that?" asked Julie.

"Yes, it does," said Father. Then he read James 3:5,6 to Julie.

Julie was sure that she did not want to start a forest fire with what she said. Don't you think she was a little more careful with her words after that?

A Little Talk about God and You

1. Do you remember the story about the sentry at our mouth? Do you think God should be that sentry? Would He keep us from saying foolish things? Would He help us to watch our words so that we don't hurt someone with them?
2. How do words hurt other people? What should we ask God to help us do about careless words that could hurt others?

BIBLE READING: James 3:1-8.
BIBLE TRUTH: Our tongue is like a fire. It can burn us and other people. From James 3:5,6.
PRAYER: Dear God, I really do not want to hurt anyone with what I say. Remind me to be kind when I want to say unkind words. Amen.

Would You Like to Make a World?

Scott had never worked with modeling clay before. "This is so much fun!" he said. "But what shall I make next?"

"Would you like to make a world?" Grandfather asked.

Scott looked surprised. "How do I do that?" he asked.

A Little Talk about Creation

1. Can you make a world? Can you make real sheep and cows and dogs? Can you make trees and grass and clouds and sunshine? Why not?
2. What do you think Grandfather will say to Scott?

"Let's try," said Grandfather. "I will help you. What shall we make first? Would you like to make an ocean or a mountain? Or should we do a waterfall or a sunset?"

Scott sat there with his mouth open. "Could we do that?" he asked.

Grandfather kept on talking. "Then we will make a rainbow and ten thousand snowflakes of different kinds. After that we will make a real live person."

"We can't do all those things," said Scott.

"Okay, we will let those things come out of this glob of clay all by themselves," said Father.

"You're kidding!" said Scott. "They couldn't possibly do that!"

"You're right," said Grandfather. "But some people say all these wonderful things just happened. They just came out of nothing all by themselves."

Scott laughed. "I'm glad the Bible tells us what really happened," he said.

"I'm glad for that too," said Grandfather. "Now why don't we make something with the clay that we really can make? That sounds like a good idea, doesn't it?"

A Little Talk about God and You

1. Why did Scott say that those things could not happen? Could anyone but God make any of those wonderful things?
2. Who made you? Does that make you special to God?
3. Have you ever thanked God for making all the wonderful things you enjoy? Would you like to do that now?

BIBLE READING: Genesis 1:1; 2:1-7.
BIBLE TRUTH: In the beginning God made the heavens and the earth. From Genesis 1:1.
PRAYER: Dear God, thank You for rainbows and sunsets and clouds and waterfalls. Thank You for making the world and everything in it. Thank You for making me. Amen.

Helping Someone Who Is Alone

"Oh, no!" said Father. "Look at this! Poor old Mrs. Turnbull fell at home and hurt herself. No one was with her and she couldn't get to a phone."

Mother looked at the newspaper that Father was reading. "Poor Mrs. Turnbull—if only we had known," said Mother. "Is she all right?"

"Someone found her, and she is better now," he answered. "She is in Memorial Hospital."

Paul looked at the newspaper too. He saw Mrs. Turnbull's picture.

"I go past her house every day on the way home from school," said Paul. "She was lying there hurting when I went by her house and I didn't even know it." Paul looked so sad that Mother and Father felt sorry for him.

Then Paul smiled. "I have an idea!" he said. "I know how I can help Mrs. Turnbull."

A Little Talk about Helping People Who are Alone

1. Do you feel sorry for Mrs. Turnbull? Why couldn't she get help?
2. What do you think Paul's idea is? Do you have any good ideas about helping Mrs. Turnbull?

"When Mrs. Turnbull gets home, I will stop at her house each day," said Paul. "I will ask her if everything is all right."

Mother and Father both smiled. "That would be a wonderful thing to do," said Father.

"She will look forward to that," said Mother. "That will be the best part of her day. She won't really be alone when you do that."

Paul could hardly wait for Mrs. Turnbull to get home. It would be fun to help her.

A Little Talk about Jesus and You

1. Why does Jesus want us to help people who cannot help themselves?
2. Is there someone like Mrs. Turnbull whom you could help? What could you do for that person?

BIBLE READING: Matthew 25:34-40.
BIBLE TRUTH: Pity the person who falls down and has no one to help him up. From Ecclesiastes 4:10.
PRAYER: Dear Lord, if there is someone who needs me, help me know what to do. Then help me do it. Amen.

Who's First?

"I'm first!" said Tom.

"No, I'm first!" said Ned.

Tom said some things to Ned that he should not have said. Then Ned said some things to Tom that he should not have said. Before long, Tom and Ned were quarreling.

"Stop!" said Mother. Then Mother talked with Tom and Ned about who should be first.

A Little Talk about Being First

1. Have you ever said "I'm first"? Has anyone ever said that to you? What happened then?
2. What do you think Jesus would say? What do you think Mother said?

"One day a woman came to see Jesus," Mother told Tom and Ned. "She was the mother of James and John, two of Jesus' disciples. She wanted Jesus to put her two sons first, ahead of all the other disciples."

"What did Jesus do?" asked Ned.

"He told the woman that His friends should not push into first place," said Mother. "If they want to be first, there is a better way—His way."

"What is that?" asked Tom.

"Jesus said we should help others," said Mother. "That is the way to be first."

Tom smiled at Ned, and Ned smiled at Tom. "Okay, you be first," said Tom.

"No, you be first," said Ned.

Mother smiled. Now Tom and Ned were having fun together!

A Little Talk about Jesus and You

1. What did the mother of James and John want Jesus to do? Why did He not do it?
2. What did Jesus say that we should do to be first? Do you think Tom and Ned were happier quarreling or helping? Why?
3. What will you remember the next time you want to be first?

BIBLE READING: Matthew 20:20-28.
BIBLE TRUTH: Whoever wants to be first must serve the other. From Matthew 20:27.
PRAYER: Sometimes I want to be first, dear Jesus. Help me remember what You said and put the other person first. Amen.

Little Can Be Big

"But that is so little!" Mary said to Father. He was showing Mary a very small key on a chain.

"Little can sometimes be big," Father answered. "Why don't we have a guessing game about this key. What important thing does this key do? You have three guesses."

A Little Talk about Small Things

1. Would you like to guess with Mary? What are three important things the key could do?
2. Think of three very small things. Do you think any of them is very important? Which one? What does it do? Why is that so important?

"What are your three guesses?" Father asked Mary.

"That key could unlock a door of our car," said Mary. "Or it could wind up a clock."

"Good," said Father. "Those are two good guesses. Both are important. But they do not tell what this key does. You have one more guess."

"It could unlock your suitcase," said Mary.

"Another good guess," said Father. "But this key does something else."

Father took a pretty little box from his

closet. He put the key in the bottom of the box and wound it. Then he opened the lid of the box. It began to play a song.

"How beautiful!" said Mary. "The box would not play music without the key, would it?"

"No, it wouldn't," said Father. "Sometimes we think we're not important because we are small, or we are not famous, or we are not rich. But God can do some beautiful things with us, just like we can with this key."

"Can God do good things through a little girl like me?" asked Mary.

"Yes," said Father. "Why don't we make a list of those good things right now?"

A Little Talk about God and You

1. What do you think Father and Mary put on their list? What are some good things you can do for God?
2. Make a list like the one Father and Mary made. Ask Father or Mother to help you. Put the list in your room. Ask God to help with one thing on the list each day.

BIBLE READING: Matthew 13:31,32.
BIBLE TRUTH: A very small seed can become a very large plant. A very small person can become very important. From Matthew 13:32.
PRAYER: Dear Jesus, sometimes I seem so little and You seem so big. Remind me to be like the little mustard seed and do something big for You. Amen.

What Do You Like to Smell?

Have you ever thought about your favorite scent? What do you like to smell most? Is it a rose or a tulip in the springtime? Is it turkey and stuffing baking in Mother's oven on Thanksgiving Day? Or is it chocolate cookies that Grandmother is baking?

What if you could not smell anything? What would you lose? Would you like to think about this?

A Little Talk about Smell

1. Would you like to make a list of ten favorite smells? What are they?
2. Which is your favorite of all?

Where did each of your favorite smells get its scent? Did any of them get it without God's help?

Perhaps you would like to talk more about this wonderful gift with Mother and Father. Remember this the next time you take a hike or go somewhere together.

A Little Talk about God and You

1. Who made your body? Who gave you special gifts to see, to hear, to touch, to taste, and to smell?

2. Can you think of any wonderful scent that God did not give? There isn't one, is there?
3. Would you like to thank God right now for this wonderful gift of smell?

BIBLE READING: 2 Corinthians 2:14,15.
BIBLE TRUTH: If God made your whole body to be one big ear, how could you smell anything? From 1 Corinthians 12:17.
PRAYER: Thank You, dear God, for that wonderful gift of smell. I know that You made me this way, and I want to love You for it. Amen.

Does It Pay to Be Courteous?

Mother knew something was wrong the minute Mike walked into the house. "What is it?" she asked. "Is something wrong?"

"When my friends and I got on the bus downtown we all sat down," Mike said. "There were plenty of seats. But when the seats were gone, a lady got on with her arms full of packages. I gave her my seat. But a couple of my friends laughed at me. They said it doesn't pay to do that. You never get anything for it. Is that true?"

A Little Talk about Courtesy

1. What would you say to Mike when he gave the lady his seat? Do you like what he did? Why?
2. What would you tell Mike if you were Mother? Does it pay to be courteous or polite?

"That depends on the kind of pay you want," said Mother. "I hope the lady did not give you money for being courteous. It would be no fun to be courteous for money, would it?"

Mike shook his head "No." He certainly would not want to be paid to be polite.

"So what other reward do we want when we are courteous to someone?" asked Mother.

"The lady was so thankful," said Mike. "She thanked me for being polite. She even smiled at me a few times on the way home."

"Would you rather have her thank you and smile than get some money?" Mother asked.

"Oh, yes," said Mike. "I felt happy about that all the way home."

"That's the other reward," said Mother. "It made you happy. Do you suppose it made someone else happy too?"

"I think Jesus is happy too," said Mike.

"If the lady is happy, you're happy and Jesus is happy, then don't worry if a friend or two laughs," said Mother.

A Little Talk about Jesus and You

1. Why would Jesus be happy to see Mike give up his seat to the lady? Does Jesus care if we are courteous or not? Why?
2. What did you do today that pleased Jesus?

BIBLE READING: 1 Peter 3:8,9.
BIBLE TRUTH: Live together peacefully and be courteous and humble. From 1 Peter 3:8.
PRAYER: Dear Jesus, let me treat other people the way I would like for them to treat me. Amen.

Jesus the Lamb

"Why does the Bible call Jesus a lamb?" Kurt asked.

Father smiled. "It does seem strange," he said, "but there was a good reason. Have you learned about burnt offerings in Sunday school?"

"A little," said Kurt, "but tell me some more."

A Little Talk about Jesus the Lamb

1. Do you know why the Bible calls Jesus a lamb?
2. What should Father say to Kurt? How did people in Old Testament times offer lambs on altars?

"In Old Testament times people would kill a lamb and burn its meat on an altar," said Father. "God told them to do this. It was their way of saying they were sorry for their sins. And it was also a way of asking God to forgive them."

"We don't do that anymore, do we?" asked Kurt.

"No, we don't need to," said Father. "When Jesus died on the cross it was the same as a very special lamb dying on a very special altar. Instead of each of us killing hundreds of lambs for our sins, Jesus became one lamb dying for all our sins. So now we ask Jesus to forgive our sins."

"I will think of Jesus the lamb every time I see a picture of lambs," said Kurt. "And I will think of the way He died for me."

A Little Talk about Jesus and You

1. How is Jesus like a lamb? What did Father say?
2. Have you asked Jesus to forgive your sins? Have you asked Him to be your Savior? If not, would you like to do that right now?

BIBLE READING: John 1:29,35,36.
BIBLE TRUTH: Jesus is the Lamb of God, who takes away the sin of the world. From John 1:29.
PRAYER: Dear Jesus, thank You for dying for my sin. I ask You to forgive my sin and be my Savior. Amen.

Temper Tantrums and Broken Towers

Craig had tried six times to put the blocks together. Each time the tower fell down.

The seventh time that the tower fell down, Craig rolled on the floor. He pounded the floor with his fists. And he said some things that good tower-builders should never say.

"Hmm," said Grandmother. "Seems to me the tower-builder looks just like his tower."

Craig stopped rolling on the floor. He stopped saying nasty things.

"What do you mean?" Craig asked.

"The Bible tells us about your tower and you. It tells us what happened to your tower and you," said Grandmother.

Craig looked surprised. "It does? What does it say about me and my tower?" he asked.

A Little Talk about Temper Tantrums

1. Have you ever had a temper tantrum? What happened? How did you feel after you did this?
2. What's wrong with a temper tantrum? Why should boys and girls not have them?
3. If you were Grandmother, what would you say to Craig about temper tantrums?

"Proverbs 25:28 tells us about you and your tower," said Grandmother. "It says that a person who can't control himself is like the walls of a city that are broken down. That's another way of saying that a boy who can't control himself is like his tower that has fallen down."

Craig looked at his tower that had fallen on the floor. It was a mess. He had worked so hard to put it together just right, but now many of the pieces had fallen apart. It didn't look much like the tower he had planned so carefully.

"I don't want to be like that messed-up tower," said Craig. "I want to be more like the tower before it fell. I'm going to ask Jesus to help me control my temper from now on."

A Little Talk about Jesus and You

1. Why didn't Craig want to be like his messed-up tower? Would you?
2. What did Craig want Jesus to help him do? Do you want Jesus to help you control your temper? Why not ask Him now.

BIBLE READING: Proverbs 25:28.
BIBLE TRUTH: A person who has a temper tantrum is like a city with its walls broken down. From Proverbs 25:28.
PRAYER: Dear Jesus, I don't want to be like a broken wall. I don't want to be like a tower that fell down. Help me control my temper, the way You would. Amen.

Where Do We Get Love?

"Look at this," Betsy said to her father. When Betsy said, "I love you, puppy," her puppy wagged his tail.

"He knows that I love him," said Betsy. "But he can't talk. How does he know?"

A Little Talk about Love

1. When you say something nice to your puppy, does he wag his tail? Do you think your puppy loves you?
2. Where does love come from? What do you think Father will say to Betsy?

"God gives a special love to each of us," said Father. "He gave you and me a love for each other. And He gave Mother and me a different kind of love for each other."

Betsy smiled. She knew that Father loved her and Mother. But she knew it was a different kind of love for Mother.

"God also gave you a different kind of love for your puppy," said Father. "And He gave your puppy a special kind of love for you. But each of these different kinds of love came from God."

"He must be a wonderful God to give us so many different kinds of love!" said Betsy.

"He is," said Father. "That's why we have a special kind of love for Him."

A Little Talk about God and You

1. Do you love your puppy or kitty differently from the way you love Mother or Father? Do you love God differently from parents or pets?
2. Where does love come from? Who gives it to us?

BIBLE READING: 1 John 4:7-11.
BIBLE TRUTH: Love comes from God. From 1 John 4:7.
PRAYER: Dear God, I love You. And I know You love me too. Amen.

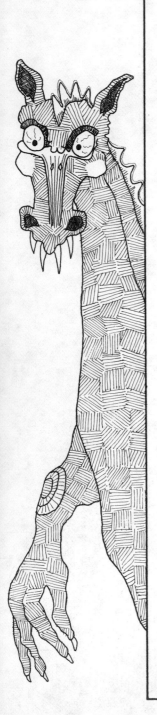

The Dragon

"Look at that mean dragon!" said Ralph. He pointed to a big stuffed dragon in the parade. Its teeth were long and sharp, and it had mean-looking eyes. It didn't look kind at all.

"Have you ever met any other dragons?" Father asked.

Ralph looked surprised. Then he began to think. What do you suppose Ralph will say?

A Little Talk about Being Mean

1. Did the dragon look kind or mean?
2. What do you think Father meant when he asked Ralph if he had met any other dragons? Have you?
3. What do you think Ralph will say to Father? What would you say if you were Ralph?

"I've seen friends who act like mean dragons," said Ralph. "They try to be cross and angry, and try to hurt other people instead of help them."

"What would you like to say to those friends?" Father asked.

"I guess I would like to tell them to stop acting like dragons," said Ralph. "No one wants to be friends with a mean dragon."

"That's good for us to remember too, isn't it?" Father asked.

"Yes, I suppose it is," said Ralph. "Jesus doesn't want us to act like mean old dragons, does He?"

A Little Talk about Jesus and You

1. Why doesn't Jesus want us to act like mean old dragons? Does He ever act that way? If He doesn't, why should we?
2. How should Jesus' friends be? Should we be kind? What would Jesus want?

BIBLE READING: 1 Thessalonians 5:15-18.
BIBLE TRUTH: Always try to be kind to each other. From 1 Thessalonians 5:15.
PRAYER: Dear Jesus, You are kind and loving and helpful. Let me be more like You each day. Amen.

Be Courteous

"I don't believe it!" said Mother. "Look at that woman cut into the middle of the line!"

Audrey looked at the woman. She could not believe it either. Her mother would never do that.

"She should be ashamed of herself," said Audrey. "That's rude. I'd like to tell her that she's rude."

"No, let's not do that," said Mother. "It would only start a quarrel. Perhaps she is in a hurry to get somewhere. We will forgive her, won't we? I can wait another two minutes to pay for my groceries."

A Little Talk about Being Courteous

1. What would you like to say to that woman who cut into the line at the grocery store? Have you ever seen people do rude things like that?
2. Do you always try to be courteous to other people? What are some special things you can do to be courteous to others? What are some rude things you should not do?

When Audrey and Mother came home and put the groceries away, they sat down at the kitchen table.

"Let's make a list of some courteous things that a girl like you can do," said Mother. "Then let's make a list of rude things that a girl like you should not do."

Audrey and Mother came up with two long lists. Do you suppose they have lists like yours?

A Little Talk about Jesus and You

1. Why should Christians be courteous? Why would Jesus want that?
2. Think of three Christian men or women whom you like very much. Are they courteous?
3. Think of someone you hope to be like when you grow up. Is that person courteous?

BIBLE READING: 1 Peter 3:8-12.
BIBLE TRUTH: Be courteous. From 1 Peter 3:8.
PRAYER: Lord, I want to be courteous because I know this will please You and others who watch me. Amen.

Will God Ever Die?

"Will God ever die?" Danny asked.

Father smiled. "Why do you ask?" he said.

"Well, if God has been here since the world began, He must be very old," said Danny. "If He is getting older, doesn't that mean He will die?"

"That would seem to be right," said Father, "but only if you are talking about one of us. We get old and die. But God does not get any older. Do you know why?"

A Little Talk about Living Forever

1. Were you a day younger yesterday? Will you be a day older tomorrow?
2. Look at a calendar. Time is measured in many different ways. Can you name some of them? (Examples: minutes, hours, days, weeks, months, years.) Do you think we will have any of those in heaven? Why not?

"God made time to help us measure our life on earth," said Father. "When we go to live in His home we will not need watches or clocks or calendars anymore. Time will not be measured as it is here on earth."

"Does that mean we will not get older in heaven?" asked Danny. "And if we don't get older, will we never really die?"

"That's right," said Father. "The Bible calls that eternal life. 'Eternal' means 'without end.' This means that God never gets old. He is always the same age."

Danny smiled. "I'm glad we can live with God in His home forever," he said.

A Little Talk about God and You

1. Will God ever die? Read 1 Timothy 1:17. "Eternal" and "immortal" means that God lives forever. He never dies.
2. Will God give us a life that never ends if we believe in Jesus? Read John 3:16. What does that say?
3. Have you asked Jesus to forgive your sins and give you eternal life? If not, why not now?

BIBLE READING: John 14:1-4.
BIBLE TRUTH: God is always the same. He never gets older. From Psalm 102:27 and Hebrews 13:8.
PRAYER: Thank You, God, for Your wonderful home that needs no watches or clocks or calendars. Please get my room ready so I can live with You someday. Amen.

What a Wonderful God!

A boy watched the thunderstorm coming. He stared at the thunderheads that seemed to reach all the way to heaven. They looked like mountains rising out of mountains, with more mountains above them. Lightning flashed. Thunder rumbled. Winds blew. It was almost too much for the boy to take in.

"What a wonderful God to make the thunderstorm!" said the boy.

A girl watched the evening sunset after the storm. The sky was streaked with every color she had ever seen, and even more. Brilliant rays of sunlight reached high into the sky. They painted the big clouds of the storm that had passed. A rainbow arched over the place where the storm clouds moved. Everything was fresh and new after the rain. It was almost too much for the girl to take in.

"What a wonderful God to make the sunset!" said the girl.

Inside the house Mother and Father looked at their new baby. A beautiful smile came upon the baby's face. Then he cooed. It was almost too much for Mother and Father to take in.

"What a wonderful God to make a baby!" said Mother.

A Little Talk about a Wonderful God

1. What is the most wonderful thing that God has given to you? He is a wonderful God, isn't He?
2. What is the most wonderful thing you have seen in God's world? He is a wonderful God, isn't He?

Tonight, before you go to bed, will you tell God how much you love Him? Will you tell Him how wonderful you think He is? He will be glad that you do.

A Little Talk about God and You

1. Read the Bible reading below, or ask Mother or Father to read it to you. Talk together about how wonderful God is.
2. Would you like to say "Praise be to You, O Lord" three times? It's good to say that often during the day, isn't it?

BIBLE READING: 1 Chronicles 29:10-13.
BIBLE TRUTH: The Lord is great, and powerful, and majestic, and filled with glory. From 1 Chronicles 29:11.
PRAYER: Praise be to You, O Lord, for You are a wonderful God. Thank You for loving me. Amen.

How to Handle Trouble

Father was talking with his two boys. "What is the best way to handle trouble?" he asked them.

"I know," said one boy. "Don't do anything. If you never do anything, then you won't get into trouble."

"No, that's not the way to do it," said the other boy. "We must keep on doing what we think is right, but ask God to help us handle trouble when it comes."

A Little Talk about Trouble

1. Which boy had the right way to handle trouble? Should you stop doing everything? Or should you ask God to help you handle trouble when it comes?
2. If you never did anything, how could you do what pleases God?

"Do you remember that rusty old car we saw when we went by the junkyard?" Father asked. "It stopped doing what it was made to do. That's why it looked that way. If we stop doing what God made us to do, we can become like that rusty old car."

"I don't want to be like that," said one boy.

"I don't either," said the other boy.

"Perhaps you would rather be like **our** car," said Father. "It does many wonderful things for us, and takes us to many wonderful places. But sometimes I have to get it fixed. A man who knows all about that car takes care of it. Then it is ready to do more wonderful things for us."

A Little Talk about God and You

1. What if Father put the family car in the garage and never used it? What would happen to it? Would it help the family go to many wonderful places? Would it be doing what it was made to do?

2. Is it better to let your car do what it was made to do and then fix it when trouble comes? Does God want you to do nothing or to do what He made you to do? Will He help you "fix" your troubles when they come? Do you ask Him to do that when you have troubles?

BIBLE READING: Psalm 46:1-3.
BIBLE TRUTH: God is our refuge and strength. He will always help us when we get into trouble. From Psalm 46:1.
PRAYER: Dear God, I don't want to hide in a closet and do nothing. And I know You don't want me to do that either. Amen.

Topical and Biblical Guide

TOPICAL GUIDE

AFRAID: What should we do when we are afraid? Little Talk 63
John 10:4,14-16

AFRAID: Who can help us most when we are afraid? Little Talk 36
Job 35:10,11

ANGELS: Do angels take care of us? Little Talk 21
Psalm 91:11, Hebrews 13:1-3

ANGER: How can we turn our anger into love? Little Talk 15
Colossians 3:12-14

ANGER: What should we do with it? Little Talk 94
Proverbs 25:28

ASHAMED: What should we do when we are ashamed of Little Talk 4
our house?
Hebrews 3:2-4

BAD: Don't call bad things good! Little Talk 70
Isaiah 5:20,21

BIBLE: How is the Bible like a lamp? Little Talk 67
Psalm 119:105; 2 Peter 1:19-21

BIBLE: How much is it worth? Little Talk 38
Psalm 19:7-10

BIG: How big is Jesus? Little Talk 65
Matthew 8:23-27

BRAGGING: How can bragging hurt us? Little Talk 84
Luke 14:8-11

CARE, GOD'S: How does God take care of us? Little Talk 75
Psalm 121:2-5

CAREFUL, BEING: Why must we be careful? Little Talk 11
Romans 14:12

CHEATING: Why should we not cheat others? Little Talk 51
Philippians 4:8,9

CHEERFULNESS: How can we help others be cheerful? Little Talk 5
Proverbs 15:13,15,30

CHEERFULNESS: God wants us to be cheerful givers. Little Talk 83
2 Corinthians 9:6-8

CHURCH: Learning to love our church and Sunday school. Little Talk 80
Psalm 122:1

CLEAN: How do we get our hearts clean? Little Talk 77
Psalm 51:10; Matthew 23:25,26

CLOTHING: Learning to be thankful for our clothing. Little Talk 56
Matthew 6:28-34

BIBLICAL GUIDE

Genesis 1:1   Little Talk 87
CREATION: Who could make a world?

Genesis 1:1-25   Little Talk 3
CREATION: Did God make everything?

Genesis 1:29,30   Little Talk 24
THANKFULNESS: Remembering to thank God for food.

Genesis 2:1-7   Little Talk 87
CREATION: Who could make a world?

Genesis 2:4   Little Talk 61
GOD: How do we know He is there?

Genesis 8:20-22   Little Talk 50
PROMISES, GOD'S: Does God keep His promises?

Exodus 33:17   Little Talk 66
NAME: Does God know my name?

Exodus 33:19   Little Talk 78
GOD'S GIFTS: He sends them like a parade before us.

Deuteronomy 33:27   Little Talk 62
COMFORT: How does God comfort us like a father?

Joshua 23:14   Little Talk 18
PROMISES: Why should we keep promises?

Ruth 1:16-18   Little Talk 57
LOYALTY: Why should we be loyal?

1 Chronicles 29:10-13   Little Talk 99
GOD: God is great and majestic

Job 6:24,25   Little Talk 59
QUIETNESS: How can we learn more by being quiet?

Job 35:10,11   Little Talk 36
AFRAID: Who can help us most when we are afraid?
COMFORT: Getting comfort from our parents.

Psalm 4:6,7   Little Talk 76
HAPPINESS: How can I share my happiness?

Psalm 16:6   Little Talk 69
GIFTS: What are the best gifts parents can give?

Psalm 19:1-4   Little Talk 9
PRAISING GOD: Why should we praise God?

Psalm 19:7-10   Little Talk 38
BIBLE: How much is it worth?

Psalm 25:8-10   Little Talk 39
GOD'S WAYS: God's ways are different from our ways.